The Friendship Tree

For Siobhán, Mary, Stephen and James.

THE FRIENDSHIP TREE

The Life and Poems of Davoren Hanna

JACK HANNA

NEW
ISLAND
BOOKS

The Friendship Tree
is first published in 1996
in Ireland by
New Island Books,
2 Brookside,
Dundrum Road,
Dublin 14,
Ireland.

ISBN 1 874597 38 3

The author and publishers would like to thank the following for permission to use
the photographs reproduced in the book: Brian Farrell, *Independent Newspapers*,
Austin Finn, Pat Cashman, Ann Egan, *Woman's Way*, the *Irish Times*,
and Colm Keating.

Grant-aided by the
Arts Council

New Island Books receives financial assistance from
The Arts Council (An Chomhairle Ealaíon),
Dublin, Ireland.

Cover design by Jon Berkeley
Typeset by Graphic Resources
Printed in Ireland by Colour Books, Ltd.

Contents

Foreword

Jack Hanna has written a loving, thoughtful and moving book about his poet-son Davoren who was physically disabled, intellectually adventurous and imaginatively brilliant. *The Friendship Tree* is one of the most incisive and humane books I have read for years. Many people will find it, as I have, a source of pure inspiration.

In essence, this is a story about three people. Davoren himself is at the centre, a gifted, cunning, resourceful and often ruthless poet who, with a disabled body, had to do justice in language to the turbulence and wonder within him.

Then there is Brighid, his mother, a lover of poetry and music, a sharp, kind, intelligent woman who could look through you in a conversation. She probed, questioned passionately, accepted gracefully what life sent her. I think it is not an overstatement to say that she gave her life to, and for, Davoren.

Thirdly, there is Jack Hanna himself—a philosopher, journalist, writer, something of a loner, chronicler of the sufferings and achievements of his son's brief years. I have always thought that Davoren Hanna was the genius-child of gifted parents. Davoren himself was aware of this and has said as much in various poems. It is absolutely right that this book should be called *The Friendship Tree* because, at its deepest level, that's what it is about: the loving friendship between these three people; the friendship between the Hanna family and many other people; the friendship between Davoren and his various helpers, those unselfish people who gave their time and talent to that magnetic boy who, though wordless, could enchant fluent talkers.

Jack Hanna's book moves effectively backwards and forwards through time. He deals with suffering and pain, with love and frustration and disappointment, with hidden thoughts and public utterances. He describes the 'explosion of manic energy' in Davoren's body when the youngster sensed his own gifts. Yet, all through the book, Jack Hanna is detached and accurate as only a truly philosophical writer can be. There isn't a sentimental line in the entire work. It is candid, accurate and severely faithful in its memories.

Under it all, and running through it, is the spirit of the poetry of Davoren Hanna. I read his poems for the TV documentary on his life, 'Poised for Flight'. As I read these marvellous poems, I was struck by their anger, wonder, gratitude, fierce power of perception and observation as well as their spirit of aspiration, flight and praise. Davoren could see the sadness in the 'young wasted faces' of our streets today; he knew the desolating impact of 'grey thoughts' making 'grey my heart'; he witnessed and celebrated the savagery and sensuality of nature; and he listened always to that music which 'hungers for hearing'. It is my belief that this book will be read and heard by all who hunger for an affirmation of that strange and wonderful human ability to turn suffering into poetry and painful human disability into singing dignity. Let me end with the four-line poem by Davoren, the title of which is also the title of this memorable book:

The Friendship Tree

There springs water, sweet water,
in my parched little plot;
greenly my soul shoots
till it brushes heaven's underbelly.

Brendan Kennelly
July 1996

Acknowledgements

At a celebration of music and poetry held in the restored curvilinear glasshouse in the National Botanic Gardens in Glasnevin on 19th November 1995, I read some of Davoren's poems. I also recited a litany of names of girls who had brought Davoren on walks in the Botanics from babyhood to adulthood. Without any straining of my memory, I came up with twenty-two names, to which I then added the names of a few of his male friends and helpers for good measure.

This book could have very fittingly been a beautiful litany of names and attributes ('weaver of dreams', 'shaft of sunlight' and 'wave of optimism' are just some of Davoren's phrases that come casually to mind) of all those who graced his life with their love, intelligence, patience and humour. But I could only tell a small fraction of the stories and dramas which marked Davoren's short life, and the reader might have become confused by such a densely peopled narrative.

I have planted this 'Friendship Tree' primarily to celebrate and remember the lives of Davoren and Brighid, but also as a gesture of thanks to all, named and unnamed, who came into our lives and sustained us. It is important to state that many of those who are not named in the book merit as much appreciation as those who feature in my recollection of Davoren's story. Friends who were with us during the hidden years when nothing seemed to be happening in Davoren's life, helpers, care-workers, nurses and therapists who quietly and self-effacingly spent time with him when he was hanging onto life by a thread — all of these deserve a chant of praise in my litany. People, some known and some unknown to me, who helped us financially — I thank them also.

Whatever interludes of dignity, flourishing and happiness emerged in Davoren's difficult life were only possible because of an immense

Acknowledgements

reservoir of care and nurture overflowing into the lives of Davoren, Brighid and myself. Without naming them, I would also like to thank friends who stood by me at a personal level, friends who were concerned to shield my life from the tragedy that befell Brighid's.

I conclude with some thanks to people who assisted me in the writing of the book. Thanks to Sinéad Brennan, who lightened my load in wading through the mounds of paper in Davoren and Brighid's records — to Cian Cafferky, Brian Lynch, Peter Jankowsky and Barry Gleeson, who read the manuscript and offered helpful suggestions — to David Vernon and Mary and John Hanna for technical assistance with computer disks — to Tom Coogan for help with photographs — and to Niamh Digan for help with translations from the Irish. My thanks and solidarity to my former *Irish Press* colleagues, always ready with an encouraging word when morale was ebbing. Denis Dermody, who lived in Bantry Road during a winter when I was often downcast, contrived to ignore my moodiness, while Brita and Rosemary helped keep me breathing and relaxed in the present when the task of reliving and writing about the past was churning me up. Margaret Gleeson offered me clear-eyed love and companionship while I tunnelled in the dark, mysterious roots of 'The Friendship Tree'.

I would like to thank Brendan Kennelly for once again lending his voice in support of that poet and rascal Davoren Hanna. My thanks to Dermot Bolger, who gently encouraged me to write a memoir of Davoren, and to publish a new edition of his poems, and to Tony Glavin, who took a keenly intelligent and warm interest in the whole project. I take full responsibility for any errors or omissions in this attempt to honour Davoren and Brighid.

Jack Hanna
7 May 1996

Astounded to Have Been There

Davoren Hanna was born in great travail, with a broken arm and fractured collar-bone, on 12th March 1975. He died peacefully in his sleep on 18th July 1994. In between he suffered and achieved depths and heights beyond the imagining of most of us. He had no speech and very little physical movement and control. He had to endure searing frustration and pain for considerable periods of his life. Yet he had a powerful 'voice' through his typed communication and poems. He had also a magnetic charm and capacity for friendship and was the inspiring centre of a very intense universe of love and solidarity.

The gateway to Davoren's voice and personality was opened by his mother Brighid, who was a very gifted individual in her own right. Sitting in his chair, Davoren was inert and almost helpless. But on Brighid's lap (first of all — and later on other laps; but make no mistake: Brighid's was the primary fulcrum), on that "fertile, museful lap" in front of his letter-board, Davoren was a fierce, wilful and insistent presence.

Brighid's death on 8th July 1990, just four years prior to Davoren's, left him stricken but not broken. The strain of working with Davoren, as he grew taller and heavier, had been taking an increasing toll on Brighid's health. Her death was sudden and devastating for us both, but I had known in my heart and soul for some time that Davoren's communication lifeline was under increasing strain. I could occasionally coax a few words out of him at his letter-board and Brighid had trained several of his helpers to type with him but none of them were working full-time with him at the time of her death.

Davoren loved unashamedly the recognition that his writing brought him. As a public personality, Davoren was sailing upon a "crest of happiness" at the time of Brighid's death. His short collection of poems,

Not Common Speech, had been published that spring and he had won several literary awards (most of them in open competitions for young writers). He had appeared twice on 'Kenny Live' and had even been interviewed on radio, typing short cryptic answers for Mike Murphy during breaks in the programme. RTÉ had just finished filming a documentary on his story, 'Poised for Flight'.

With Brighid's sudden death on the night of the World Cup final, after the fortnight of Ireland's heady exploits in Italy, a jaunty Davoren was dashed to the ground. With my help and that of our friends and helpers, Davoren had to rebuild his life which had depended so much on Brighid being his mediator. I use the strong phrase 'rebuild his life' in order to make it clear that, despite the enormity of Davoren's handicap, he was never just the passive recipient of care. Davoren was a great supporter, encourager and inciter of those in his circle. I can honestly say that Davoren's strength after his mother's death played a big part in keeping my heart up during the years that followed.

I had always been more impressed by the forcefulness of Davoren's personality than by his public achievements as a poet and celebrity. His poems can speak for themselves and other writers, such as Brendan Kennelly in his introduction, can assess that public voice, but behind that limelight life of Davoren lay a hidden chronicle of harrowing struggle and rich resources, of cruel imprisonment and daily, but tiny, leaps of liberation.

As Davoren's father, I am uniquely qualified to tell the story of this behind-the-scenes drama. As the following pages will reveal, I suffered and probably still suffer from the same mixture of blindness to, and difficulty with, the real character of their sons as most fathers do, especially during those turbulent teenage years. But because of the degree of Davoren's handicap and because of his mother's health problems and subsequent death, he and I were locked in an embrace of care and conflict of great intensity.

Even now, more than a year after Davoren's death, I don't know what to do with my arms anymore. After nineteen years of cradling, lifting, holding, massaging, comforting and hugging his body from babyhood to manhood (at the time of his death, Davoren's weight was not much more than four stone), my arms feel empty, useless, pointless. In these arms I still feel intense surges of happiness. But inscribed in them too are anguish, desolation and anger.

Apart from short holiday breaks, Davoren lived all his life at home. His nights were frequently racked by intense pain and discomfort and, as time went on, increasingly his days too. Almost as one body, we two (and when Brighid was alive, often we three) felt the tide going out very very far, the blood of hope draining from our pores. But we also experienced the exultant fullness of his triumphs. His public acclaim had of course an intoxicating effect but I'm thinking mainly of the rushes of delight which coursed through him when he communicated some impish or dramatic thought, when he felt really understood or when he was affected by a piece of music.

⌐□□⌐

Imagine an afternoon scene in the winter of 1989 when Davoren was fourteen. In the small living-room (the other downstairs room was his bedroom) between rests and tea-breaks, Davoren and Brighid were trying to type out some poem, a letter to a friend or some other 'urgent' communication. In our then tiny kitchen, I was trying to sort out the mess, both washing a few dishes and cooking a dinner before going to work. I was banging pots and pans and cursing and swearing (and remembering a time when never a foul word passed my lips). I knew that this time of straining creativity (on Brighid and Davoren's part) would have to be paid for. Brighid was facing into a long evening minding Davoren on her own. For all of us there was the night-time torments to be faced. My cup of frustration was spilling over.

Despite Davoren's 'successes' I could feel, on an afternoon like that, our lives going down the tubes. Anger and tears were often close. All the disappointments of my life (wanting other children, the pain of missing out on so many of the 'normal' joys of parenthood, my disgruntlement at my career setbacks) welled up in my offstage kitchen outpost. Try as I might to limit my displays of spleen to the pots and pans, I probably vented some of my hopelessness on Brighid and Davoren.

Out of the corner of my enraged eye, I would see upset taking hold of Davoren. I would hear a throaty, gurgly squawk. But I could also detect a shift in his pattern of movement, an extra degree of agitation in his thrashing about for the letters on his board.

I knew what was coming — a barbed but encouraging shaft to pierce the armour of my rage. I would be on my guard, ready to resist this *plámás*, these extravagantly expressed blandishments. Sometimes indeed they would add a note of guilt to my turbulence and intensify my foul humour. Eventually Davoren's words would be read out.

It distresses me to see Dada so worn out!

Royal father, take counsel from your sage. Some day you will tie garlands round your poet's head.

With a fierce effort, Davoren would lift his head and look me straight in the eye with a cheeky, expectant grin. I was disarmed. I couldn't continue my fight in the bunker and knelt to give him a hug. As I enfolded him on his perch straddled across one of Brighid's legs, his legs bicycled and he kicked me in the balls. It was a game — a longstanding game, one of our favourites. I fell back, wounded and hurt on the floor. And Davoren exploded in paroxysms of joy.

My overwhelming impression is that I was a witness, and not always a sober and equable witness, to a scale of human expression — from tortured muteness to soaring flight — beyond the common measure. 'Not Common Speech' — a phrase taken from the American Jewish poet Denise Levertov which we used as the title for his first book of poems — captures neatly one aspect of the strange, intense world which we inhabited. We shared this world with our friends and helpers. Other supporters, journalists, and the general public through the medium of television had occasional glimpses of its bewildering, tormenting and exhilarating enchantment but essentially, like all family life, it was largely a hidden world.

I was a father to this savagely handicapped but remarkably gifted young man, I was a partner to this big-hearted woman with compelling expressive talents in her own right. Now sadly I am the sole survivor from a cauldron of human experience which I even yet only dimly understand. Taking up the last line from Davoren's poem, 'Famine', I was and still am "astounded" to have been there.

Giddily Poised on the Edge

The first window that I want to open onto the 'secret' world of Davoren focusses on the last two-and-a-half months of his life. As chance would have it, I have a very precise record of a dramatic turning-point during the last phase of Davoren's short span of years. In the early hours of 29th April, 1994, I had poured out my thoughts in a letter to a friend after a day during which I had drunk deeply of the full cocktail of dejection and blessedness which living with Davoren involved. As I wrote:

> Dav and I went for a walk this afternoon in the Botanics and even though he slept most of the time, it did my heart good. At least there was no obvious distress. We saw a squirrel — which has been a good omen for me ever since we moved into this house — and I had brief interludes being entranced by the trees. This evening I got involved in digging up the back garden in the beautiful evening light. In fact the light was already fading as I began. After a while Guénaëlle brought Davoren out in his armchair and his eyes were sparkling and he was shrieking with delight. His sudden buoyancy lifted a weight of depression from my heart.

I can still vividly recall the lightness in my heart as what I would describe at his funeral as "Davoren in the full ecstasy of communication" radiated and rippled in the glow of that balmy April evening. The gates of his self-expression were flung open after a long period of being tightly shut. Davoren, my teenage son to whom I had clung in a tight tussle for survival during all of his life, was emerging as a confident, buoyant young man.

The strange thing for those who know Davoren through his poems or other written communications is that this epiphany didn't require any words. The shrieks were important, the fire in his eyes, his passion for

Guénaëlle, the piston-like thrashing of his legs which were normally locked hard in spastic rigidity — all these were part of the picture. But it was the cascade of happiness tumbling from his heart that was the real achievement of communication by Davoren on that day, and that lodged itself in my heart during the two-and-a-half months that remained to him on this earth.

You have to go back to earlier in that day to realise fully the depths and heights of Davoren. I had brought him up to Beaumont Hospital Out-Patients for a review after a fortnight which he had spent in hospital over Easter. That crisis had come at the end of a seven-month period during which he had fallen into what seemed like a terminal physical and psychological slump. In September 1993 I had to bring him to hospital in a critical condition from Richmond Cheshire Home where he was staying for a few days. In Beaumont he spent almost a week in a coma with liver complications and a chest infection. He and I were fearful that he might not pull through but with the toughness and cheerfulness he had displayed in so many struggles in the past, Davoren bounced back and came home after a fortnight.

A week later he was back in hospital with another severe infection. We spent the rest of 1993 building him back up and at the same time seeking out activities to stimulate and engage him. We tried and failed to have him accepted as an 'auditor' at Trinity College courses in English. He went in a similar capacity to St Patrick's College in Drumcondra and this roused and animated him for a week or two, but then he fell ill and had pain and discomfort in his chair and this project too had to be abandoned.

The most discouraging feature of the year was the slump in Davoren's spirits. Communication through the medium of Davoren's helpers had become excruciatingly difficult since his mother's death. Whereas his whole body had become increasingly buckled and a slight gain in weight had put an extra strain on him and his helpers, the main problem seemed to us a progressive ebbing of his morale.

A certain mood of resignation had set in. When Sorcha Saidléar, his most long-standing communication ally, came to visit, he never seemed to exhibit the same urgency to be taken on her lap and set in front of his letter-board as formerly. He would often content himself with a few words of encouragement to me and his other friends and helpers.

At the same time it had been a particularly lively year *around* Davoren. We had Céline Tessier, the fifth in a line of Breton girls who had worked as 'au pairs' with Davoren since his mother's death, and Guénaëlle Havy, who had stayed on in Ireland after a year living with us, at the centre of our lives. I often came home from work to find not just two but three or four young French women hovering around Davoren. It had been a great year for parties. There was always a birthday or someone coming or going — any excuse for a hooley. All of Davoren's Irish helpers and friends gathered regularly around him but I had a strong sense that we were often supporting each other. Davoren was in our midst, delighted to be the focus of attention, but there was also a feeling that life was closing in on him.

This was why that balmy late April evening gave such a powerful lift to my spirits. It brought me back almost a decade to those early days when Davoren first began to type out his thoughts on the keyboard with Brighid. Davoren, whom most people saw locked in spasticity in his chair, with straps and supports, regularly became an uncontrollable human dynamo on Brighid's lap. His legs kicked like pistons, he dived onto the keyboard putting an immense strain on Brighid's back and jerked his head backwards, sometimes dangerously knocking the back of his head against Brighid's mouth.

> *Were I to sail upon the crest*
> *of happiness surging in my heart,*
> *clay thoughts would crumble*
> *and my harrowed tongue be freed.*

To many of those who met Davoren only briefly or who saw only his public face, often enough distressed and strained, it is hard to convey the passion that coursed through Davoren's body in some of these private moments, the explosion of manic energy that lit up his face when what he had to 'say' was acknowledged and valued.

A particular episode that I recall occurred when Davoren was about ten and we were watching an early programme about Stephen Hawking, outlining the adventure of his cosmological ideas and the increasing difficulty of his struggle to communicate them. Davoren was in his pyjamas as we were on the countdown towards his bed-time.

About half-way through the programme, Davoren became very excited and began to thrash about to such an extent that it became very difficult for me to control this spastic child jerking and diving on my lap. The lap of his mother (occasionally mine and more frequently those of his helpers) was like what the bath was for Archimedes — the leaping-ground for his 'Eurekas'.

Brighid and I were fascinated by the programme, and could see many parallels despite the vast differences between Stephen Hawking's situation and Davoren's. We were particularly struck by a remark of Hawking about his good fortune that his speciality was the one field in physics which depended almost entirely on thought and speculation.

What happened next was entirely characteristic of Davoren's energy at that time and how it irrupted into our lives. Brighid was already tired but Davoren's excitement could not be stilled. His eyes were incandescent as he squawked and shrieked (Davoren had no speech but when excited he could make quite a racket) and his arms and legs continued to flail about.

Brighid said she would put him on her lap in front of the typewriter and allow him just one sentence. Brighid was never very rigid in imposing her limits on Davoren so I am sure he got away with more than his quota. I clearly recall that his main statement was: "At last I understand the reason for my handicap."

Still his imperious insistence continued to make itself felt. This determination often gave rise to intense battles with Brighid in which Davoren could be quite ruthless. I often thought in the wake of her death that he must have experienced terrible guilt about the strain which he imposed on Brighid — and somehow these late-night trials of strength came vividly to mind when I tried to recall that strain.

Yet that night it was not brute tenacity to impose his will that Davoren exhibited, but rather a repertoire of impish, almost sly tricks that he used to charm his way through Brighid's defences. First the right fist would nonchalantly wander over towards the top of the board where by convention Brighid and he had agreed there was a 'poem' sign. At Brighid's protests — "No, it's too late!" — he would desist for a while. Then he would commence stabbing, jerking movements towards the poem area. Then he would turn to cajolery, trying to jerk himself back so that he could kiss Brighid, brushing his head against her cheek. Whenever I would try to mediate in the conflict, he would get exceedingly animated.

That night Brighid was an open door; the level of Davoren's excitement was such that she would have needed a heart of stone to resist him. The poem/conversation/outburst which followed was very characteristic of Davoren at his most perverse, wilful, arrogant and dogmatic:

Magical Kinaesthesis

A happy quest for nature's answers
will be patiently relinquished.
Ignoring questions, geophysicists
search the atmosphere in vain.
Why this evolution occludes clarity
greatly mystifies knowledgeable minds.

As a preface to the poem, Davoren wrote 'God created the Younivers!' (I will explain Davoren's spelling and writing procedures later.) He had somehow picked up that Stephen Hawking was espousing an evolutionary view of the origins of the universe with no room for God in the picture. Whether Davoren was right in attributing this view to Stephen Hawking in the programme (my recollection is that this issue didn't really arise) scarcely matters; the point is that Davoren was fired up to make a poetic riposte to this insult to his God-centred world-view.

From my point of view there were several interesting things about Davoren's intervention. The first was that I could not deny the energy and commitment of this almost-demented ten-year-old thrashing about on his mother's knee. There was that mixture of glee and wilfulness which can be seen in any childish act of self-assertion, but in this case it was thrusting itself out to make claims in the adult worlds of philosophy, theology and poetry.

The second was that his oracular style got up my nose. As someone who had studied philosophy for most of my adult life, I considered that I had laboured hard to understand the issues involved in accommodating an evolutionary world-view within a religious or spiritual perspective, without in the end being any nearer a resolution of the matter, and I was frankly irritated by Davoren's peremptoriness and tone of certainty.

ꆔꆔꆔꆔ

That 'Hawking' evening was just one particularly vivid example of a younger Davoren at the peak of his powers that I recalled that spring of 1994, as the clouds of despondency lifted and he began to exhibit some of his old enthusiasm and cockiness. The most obvious medical sign of this resurgence was that on 28th April, the very day of our Botanics walk and his evening ecstasy, the doctors in Beaumont Hospital had recommended bringing him back the following week for blood transfusions. However, when I brought him in for admission the following Thursday, Davoren's haemoglobin blood-count had returned to normal and he was, so to speak, in the pink of condition until the day of his death.

Heartened by this change in his pallor and morale, I began to plan summer activities for Davoren. I had marked down 1994 as the year for our grand tour of the Breton connections, but the trip had fallen by the wayside because he had been so weak earlier in the year that it seemed pointless to be dragging him around France. We had made a trip to Brittany two years previously when we had two families to visit, but by 1994 we had established deep connections with four families. Somehow Jane, Sylvie, Guénaëlle and Céline had communicated to their families something of Davoren's peculiar charm and they 'fell in love' with him at a distance.

This silent magnetic charm which he exerted on Breton families was only one flowering of a capacity to open hearts which was as elemental a feature of Davoren as his poems and communications. In order to illustrate this circle of love surrounding Davoren, I now introduce two members of what came to be known as 'the siblings'.

Clíona Saidléar and Helena Boyd were friends who had started working with Davoren as young teenagers, several years before his mother's death. They had cared for Davoren but had also grown up with him. They were in fact only two or three years older than him. They understood better than anyone the need that Davoren had to get away from his father's sheltering shadow. They were continually inventive and conspiratorial in finding ways of involving him in the rough-and-tumble of life. There is no better way to describe the impact that Davoren had on Clíona's life than to reproduce what she wrote a few days after his death:

> Dearest Davoren, Bungling through my formative years, you were a light that shone brightly. You taught me to love, without quota or shame — to care, without pity or charity — to forgive, without recompense or memory — to laugh, without need for care or cause. Among many things you taught me to dream of stars beyond hope and never to be afraid to reach out to them — that hope has no limit.
>
> Eight years I sat at your knee. Now the student must bid you farewell. I thank you from my soul and humbly pray you may be proud of me.
>
> Le grá mór.
> Clíona.

Clíona was a bundle of energy whose language, English or Irish (Irish was the language of the family home), tumbled out of her in *sruthanna*. She had a long mane of chestnut hair which she tossed exuberantly, and even more spiritedly when she was dancing (there was also a strong family tradition of Irish and folk dancing). Clíona was generous and impulsive and gave herself to Davoren's life (and perforce to Brighid's and mine) in all sorts of ways that went beyond the call of duty. She had accompanied us on many trips around Ireland and had indeed assisted me willingly on many occasions when Davoren was suffering and struggling during the middle of the night. Her spirit was bright and cheerful but she could be counted on during the tough times also.

Helena's temperament and colouring were of a darker hue. Her hair was jet-black and her complexion vivid and animated. She had a critical, searching, combative intelligence and was wont to engage in intense debates with Clíona on religion, literature, films or life itself. She had worked with Davoren and me very regularly in the period after Brighid's death and had been a very steadying influence on both of us. She was wise beyond her years in discerning what we needed to see us through that difficult time.

I could do a list, somewhat like Don Giovanni's catalogue, of Davoren's women friends over the years: girls his own age, helpers somewhat older, fellow handicapped spirits, older women friends — one of Helena's jokes was to refer to our household as 'Dav's harem' — but for the moment I am letting Clíona and Helena stand for that circle of attraction that grew up around Davoren. He was the core of a powerful magnetic field pulling people into his world.

Or perhaps a more organic image captures better the ambiguity of his inexorable attraction. He was like a motionless spider drawing people into his web. Whether it was the impish smile or the haunting look in his eyes, once you fell under Davoren's spell, you didn't easily escape. As a responsible parent, I mainly appreciated the qualities of caring and gaiety which these allies brought to Davoren. While I fretted about how I could keep this 'magic ring of nurture' going for him, it only gradually dawned on me, dimwitted as fathers sometimes are, what an intoxicating brew it could be for a young man.

❑❑❑❑

An initiative which had sustained my morale earlier in that year of 1994 was the restoration of a cottage in Donegal which had been left to Davoren and myself by Brighid. It was a fairly primitive cottage situated on Mulnamina More, a hill overlooking the Gweebarra estuary in southwest Donegal. Brighid had died there of a heart attack in July four years previously and since then it had been very difficult for Davoren and myself to avail of it, with his troublesome health and the gradually deteriorating condition of the cottage, which was very inaccessible for Davoren. My mother died in January 1991 and had left me a little money, some of which I decided to spend on making the cottage more comfortable and accessible. Two of our friends, Ann Mullen and Denis Dermody, had been particularly enterprising in undertaking some of the follow-up decoration of the cottage in the depths of the winter after the building work had been completed.

Thus I was very keen to bring Davoren up to see the transformation — I felt fairly guilty about investing in the cottage when most of the time it didn't seem possible for him to make much use of it. So in May 1994, heartened by Davoren's revival, I began planning excursions to Donegal with some of the young helpers.

The first expedition was with Davoren, Céline and Denis in late May. Davoren was in very sunny form but a little bit lethargic. Perhaps the travelling had worn him out and I did too much driving around, being anxious to show Céline as much of the rugged Donegal landscape as I could before she returned to France.

The 'équipe' for the second expedition in late June was a particularly frisky one, with Guénaëlle, Clíona and Helena. Guénaëlle's boyfriend, Colm Saidléar, a brother of Clíona, joined us for a day or two. The atmosphere was uproarious from the word go, with merriment, affection and slagging vying for dominance. At a hotel near Cavan on the journey up to Donegal, the girls careered around the car park with Davoren in his chair and then prostrated themselves in all sorts of comical postures, thumbing a lift from me as I attempted to get on the road again. Helena in particular teased me mercilessly over my attempts to give a firm lead to the expedition, stroking the few hairs on the top of my head with mock soothing. Davoren got great mileage out of the torture three vivacious young women could inflict on a *fadó fadó* person like myself.

The weather on our first full day in Donegal was blissful and we went to Cruit Island, where the sand has a warm reddish hue. Davoren was passed with gay abandon from chair to lap, from shoulder to rug and then back to his chair again amid the antics on the beach.

The forecast for the second day was equally favourable but a thick haze refused to lift. I had grown increasingly irritable in the humid atmosphere around the house, whereas the young people got immersed in games, involving Davoren as much as they could. Being housebound in Donegal didn't suit me — I longed for the rugged hills and wild beaches — but I was mainly tormented by guilt. Earlier in the year, when Davoren was sluggish and I felt at the end of my tether, I had made a series of bookings for respite care for Davoren. However, I had suddenly realised that I had confused the dates and that as soon as we arrived back in Dublin, I would be dispatching him on a two-week respite stay in Cuan Aoibhean, a centre attached to St Mary's Hospital in the Phoenix Park. I didn't know whether Davoren knew what was facing him and I didn't have the heart to bring it up in the midst of the carefree holiday mood. Instead I felt like a wet blanket on Davoren's renewed vigour.

My guilt also fed into the ebb and flow of my efforts to support Davoren's dream of a greater measure of independence. The truth was that he and I had been gradually losing heart about it. The Richmond Cheshire Home in Monkstown was very sympathetic to our case and had a whole new philosophy (and building lay-out) more attuned to independence. However, on several visits there in 1993 his health had broken down. Despite these setbacks, we decided to give it another try and the week which Davoren spent there in the middle of June 1994 went spectacularly well. Members of staff, who up to this had only known Davoren in a slump, saw for the first time the buoyant personality which he could be. His friends and helpers visited him, he toured all the pubs in the vicinity and when I picked him up, he was triumphant. The avenue to greater independence seemed open again.

But during the Easter slump and subsequent hospitalisation in 1994, I had made a second respite care booking for Davoren in Cuan Aoibhean. The staffing levels and medical back-up were obviously greater in Cuan Aoibhean [translated as beautiful harbour or haven of peace] than in the Cheshire Home, so I thought Davoren would have a better chance of holding his own there. Davoren had agreed to the plan although naturally he wasn't a big fan of hospitals. Yet now in Donegal my 'respite break' chickens were coming home to roost and stirring up my guilt.

I knew the only thing that would soothe my jangled nerves was a swim so I went off to the beach on my own and plunged into the hazy sea. I then made a few phone calls to Dublin to let off some steam and did the shopping before climbing back up to the cottage to prepare the evening meal. I was still prickly but the good-natured banter of the gang softened me up. After dinner the mist cleared and we decided to head for Dooey beach. It was balmy with a hazy sunset by the time we descended to the beach at 10.30. We carried Davoren to the edge of the dunes overlooking the flat expanse of sand and the incoming waves. Clíona and Guénaëlle sat beside him with his feet dangling over the cliff. I stripped off immediately for a fresh encounter with the surf while Helena and Colm played football on the beach.

Eventually a game developed lofting kicks towards Davoren, Clíona and Guénaëlle on their sand-dune eyrie. This horseplay gave rise to much roaring and shouting, tumbling and falling, with cascades of laughter breaking over Davoren at near-misses from cannoned shots. As the darkness (which never quite becomes darkness in the West during June) descended, my abiding image of Davoren was of him living happily, giddily, perilously poised, on the edge — surrounded by his loving friends and supporters.

We adjourned to Paki's Bar at Corr Point overlooking the Gweebarra Estuary from the opposite shore to the cottage. My crisis over Davoren's coming fortnight in Cuan Aoibhean was over; I discussed it with him and the gang over a drink. There was a coming-of-age for me over those few days which mirrored Davoren's crossing of the threshold to adulthood. I had been caught for so long in this predicament with Davoren; on the one hand, he was this wilful, assertive, intelligent, spirited, challenging young man; on the other hand, he required a level of care and vigilance far beyond that demanded by a baby, from his most intimate body functions to the slightest movement. I had real blocks and difficulties communicating with this independent young man and often my best (but at the same time most painful) communication with him was when I had to enfold him on my lap like a baby to assuage the torment in his limbs or in his stomach.

Over those last few months of Davoren's life, the scales of resistance to his independent being seemed to fall gradually from my eyes. I could accept my son being able and eager for the challenges of independent living. These would be difficult explorations for him because of the degree of his handicap and often it seemed a matter of one step forwards, two steps backwards, but I could suddenly see that old fiery steel in him, the same determination that had helped him endure years of imprisonment in a world of minimal communication.

Yet to get the full picture of how it was for Davoren at the end of his short life, it is necessary to return to the scene of some of his earlier battles — when he lived for years literally "on the edge" of life and death, and with the terrible fear that his voice would never be heard.

Birth Pangs, Shock Waves

Brighid and I did not have a great store of family wisdom to fall back on when Davoren was born. Brighid's parents were dead and mine were relatively elderly and we seemed to be the first of our contemporaries to have children.

We married in June 1970 after a two-year courtship in the exciting atmosphere of the late sixties in UCD. Brighid was twenty-five and had entered the working world, already showing some of the strengths as a teacher which she was to exhibit in her professional life until the time of her death. I was twenty-three and, apart from taking some tutorials in UCD, I had no job, as I was doing post-graduate studies in philosophy. It was a passion but I was not very career-minded. We were both dreamers but Brighid was more practical. I lecturered in philosophy in the Milltown Institute of Theology and Philosophy during 1971-72 but we went for the following academic year to Paris, where Brighid was an *assistante* in a lycée while I studied and gave private lessons in English. The thoughts of having children had been in our hearts since the early days of courtship but life was full of other adventures so there didn't seem to be any rush.

Apart from our innocent, almost hippy-like, approach to life's responsibilities (we spent the afternoon of our wedding on a beach), we had an altogether more serious reason for our delay in having children. Brighid had been a diabetic since the age of eleven. During all the time I was with her, she injected herself with insulin twice daily. The care and management of childhood-onset diabetes was, and is, improving all the time; nonetheless Brighid's condition gave rise to a certain trepidation about pregnancy.

I remember vividly the occasion when Brighid told me about her diabetes. It was early days, a month or two after we got to know each other. We were taking an evening stroll in the Phoenix Park; she had something important to tell me. I had to be informed about her diabetes for all sorts of practical reasons. She needed to eat urgently fairly often in order to counteract imbalances due to the effects of the insulin in her bloodstream. But there were more than these practical motives impelling Brighid to tell me about her diabetes. She knew that her condition had long-term implications and she wanted to be absolutely fair with me.

I know that it is not the reality of diabetes care today, but at times Brighid's life was like a game of dice poised between two perils — too much insulin or too little. The most dramatic diabetes episode occurred very early, on our first visit to Donegal, before we were married. We went walking up Slieve League, those awesome cliffs in the southwest of the county. We were well stocked with food for the journey and it was a clear sunny day, but we dallied as the steep climb had taken a lot out of Brighid. By the time we started our descent on the landward side she was reduced to finishing off a large chunk of cheddar cheese. Soon after that she collapsed into a kind of alcoholic daze and I had to half-carry, half-drag her down the rest of the mountain. Outside the first house we came to, a farmer was digging his potatoes. All he could offer us was more bread and cheese with a cup of tea, but it was sufficient to revive her and, thanking him, we continued on our way.

◻◻◻◻

We always felt that Davoren's life began in Donegal — that he was conceived in the loft of a cottage we were renting overlooking Gweebarra Bay in late June 1974. In mid-July, Brighid went off to Sweden and Norway, trying to earn some money with a view to going to the Mozart Festival in Salzburg, Austria. She had to cut short her plans (which I thought were crackpot anyway) when she discovered she was pregnant. I meanwhile had stayed behind in Dublin to work and study.

During pregnancy with diabetes, the baby (which has a tendency to be larger than the norm) has to be carefully monitored, and usually has to be induced early. This took a comic turn for a few days late in 1974 when the doctors suspected that Brighid might be carrying twins. Up to then I had a somewhat bloodless picture of my impending fatherhood. Suddenly my imagination was lit up, my head peopled with images of babies moving, staring wide-eyed, babbling, gurgling and cooing. The idea of the single unique baby didn't fire me but somehow the playfulness of a multiplicity of babies generated a kaleidoscope of fantasies. The other major change in my life was that I felt I had to step out of my philosophical bubble and get a full-time job of some sort. Thus I ended up taking a job with the then Department of Posts and Telegraphs as a night telephonist.

Brighid had one diabetic crisis (a severe imbalance in her blood-sugar levels) during the pregnancy which we were assured would have no ill-effects. Then at about six-and-a-half months she developed high blood pressure and swelling in her feet and legs for which she had to rest almost continually. Somewhat belatedly Brighid had her Mozart interlude, as a friend lent us a quality stereo system and his complete collection of Mozart symphonies, which Brighid lay in bed absorbing through her pores. We often used to joke afterwards that Davoren's rapture in the presence of music (my own view is that music entered more deeply into his soul than any language) dated back to this period in his life.

Davoren's birth was induced in the National Maternity Hospital, Holles Street, on 12th March 1975, but a crisis quickly developed when it was discovered that he was a difficult shoulder presentation. He was delivered by forceps, categorised as severely traumatised, with a broken arm and a fractured collar-bone. We were ourselves traumatised by the sight of his battered condition in the intensive care unit, where we discovered a distant cousin of Brighid's, Mela Woods, who was taking care of him, and who would become a lifelong ally to all three of us.

While the medical staff understood our distress, they did not expect Davoren's injuries to cause any problems, assuring us that babies' bones healed very readily. In fact after about a month his hand had to be put in plaster as the nerves hadn't set properly but when he was reviewed by the surgeon, we were told to go away and "forget that anything ever happened to him".

In the meantime a slow, hidden, marathon battle for survival had begun for Davoren. Brighid tried to breast-feed Davoren but a combination of her discomfort after stitches and his poor sucking reflex meant that her effort had to be abandoned. We just thought we had a difficult baby on our hands as we spent hours trying to give him his bottles. He must have gained weight relatively normally as his check-ups didn't give rise to any alarm, but it was at the cost of a day-to-day struggle which we accepted as part of our new responsibilities. In fact we were rocked back on our heels as caring for Davoren took over our lives. He cried a lot but my main memory is of the hours of the day and night spent feeding him. Brighid gave up her full-time job with a hope of going back to further study when things settled down. We consoled ourselves with fond illusions of Brighid going off to lectures with Davoren snug in a pouch slung from her shoulders.

The day of Davoren's christening was a good example of the extremes of our lives at that time. There was great rejoicing among family and friends but in the midst of it all, Davoren was mainly miserable and threw up his bottle twice on the carpet of the friends' house which we had borrowed for the occasion.

The name was the big talking-point. "I suppose he could be the first St Davoren," said Fr Ben Kiely, a teacher colleague of Brighid's. Brighid was intensely proud of her Clare roots on her mother's side. Her mother, Rose Davoren, had filled her head with some of these notions and over the years we had made many pilgrimages to Cahermacnaghten, the site of the O'Davoren law school in the fourteenth-century as recorded in the Annals of the Four Masters. We had played around with various corruptions of it in case we had a girl, but when he was born, Davoren Hanna he became without any admixture or addition — a unique name for a son whose uniqueness in all sorts of ways we were on the verge of discovering.

Notwithstanding the daily toll on our energies, the spark of Davoren's spirit lit up our home. Brighid was often to remark in later years, when a diagnosis of him as being mentally handicapped was being urged upon us, how she was consoled by her memory of Davoren's first smile coming at the time recorded in all the standard baby-books (which like all inexperienced parents we dipped into fretfully). In between his sucking and feeding tussles and consequent exhaustion, Davoren showed brightness and alertness and intensity although it would be wrong to say that we noticed anything else special about him. Like all parents with a new baby, all signs of radiance shining forth from our helpless bundle were marvels to us.

When Davoren was approximately six months old, some relatives and friends (wiser and older heads than ours) were growing anxious and gently suggested that we get Davoren checked out. His failure to hold his head up was the main cause of concern. We were referred by the paediatrician in Holles Street to Dr Ciaran Barry in the Central Remedial Clinic (CRC) in Clontarf. The diagnosis on Davoren was that he probably had suffered brain damage — the terms 'spasticity' and 'cerebral palsy' were used — but that no prognosis could be made at that stage as to how he would progress.

Cerebral palsy is a developmental disability. There is nothing in the new-born baby to indicate that there is a problem. Sharper attention to Davoren's feeding difficulties might have rung alarm bells earlier, not that it would have made any difference. It is only as normal developmental milestones, such as lifting the head, crawling, babbling, eye focusing and holding of objects, come up, that the type and degree of handicap can be assessed.

Eoin O'Byrne, a young man who was a great friend to Davoren during the last five years of his life, refuses to use technical terms to describe the various 'handicapped' people he has worked with over the years. I greatly respect the wisdom in that approach. There is no doubt that medical labelling puts the emphasis on the handicapping condition rather than on the person. Nonetheless it might be useful to focus on some of the technical aspects of Davoren's disabilities in order to give some impression of the imprisoning obstacles he surmounted to communicate and write his poetry.

Davoren's physical handicap was classified as quadriplegic spastic cerebral palsy but these categories are not rigid. For instance, quadriplegia specifies that all four limbs are affected but with cerebral palsy it is not like someone who suffers a spinal injury later in life where head control may be unaffected. It might be more aptly called 'cinqueplegia' (from the

Greek: five blows) in Davoren's case, as his head control was characterised by extremes of floppiness and rigidity with various other contortions and twistings thrown in.

The spasticity in the limbs does not originate in the limbs at all, but is caused by a breakdown at the level of the brain and the central nervous system. The subtle interplay of tensing one set of muscles and relaxing another set which underlies the simplest limb movement just does not work in the case of someone affected by spasticity. Everything tenses up at the one time and in fact the greater the intensity of effort, the more likely it is that the muscles will seize up.

This feature of cerebral palsy became cruelly decisive later on in Davoren's life when we made every effort to discover some limb movement which he could consistently control. On many occasions when Davoren was relaxed, this leg movement or that arm movement would seem a promising avenue, but put into a stressful situation, he could not reproduce it.

Other types of cerebral palsy are marked by a high degree of uncontrolled movement, such as wild lunges of the arms or insistent kicking of the legs. You are often in some danger of getting a clout or a kick with several good friends of Davoren when they get excited. In Davoren's case, the frenetic thrashing of his legs of which I have already spoken, a kind of scissoring of the legs across one another, threatened to dislocate his hips. At the age of about four, surgery to cut some of the adductor muscles in the thigh was undertaken in order to avert this deformity.

Depending on its severity, the original brain malfunction can have effects throughout the body. In Davoren's case, despite intensive physiotherapy, he had severe curvature of the spine, locked limbs and deformities in his hands such that they functioned like fists rather than hands.

The lack of control is not confined to the limbs and head; it can play havoc with the muscular reflexes which co-ordinate breathing, eating, drinking, sucking and eventually speech. In fact the single greatest toll on

Davoren's energy and ours over the years was his difficulties swallowing and the tedious hours spent trying to get nourishment into him.

If we reeled in shock as we left the CRC on that fateful day of his initial diagnosis in the autumn of 1975, the corridors, clinics, school, therapy rooms and consulting rooms of the centre became regular places of pilgrimage for us over the remaining nineteen years of Davoren's life. His progress or lack of progress, his battles, defeats and victories were clinically charted and all sorts of support and back-up were provided. There was conflict too, as Brighid and I challenged later assessments of Davoren, but I now want to honour the CRC as a humane place of welcome for us with the head physiotherapist for many years, Kay Keating, being a spirited and challenging beacon for Brighid's morale in particular.

The Clinic is also a place of joy. I remember sitting on a chair in the wide corridors as the children from the school descend on the canteen for their lunch. It is like the march of the army of the crippled and the maimed (I use the strong words which have caused and still do cause me such pain when others use them). Some are on walking frames, others totter perilously, defying gravity as they lurch and stagger. Occasionally there is a fall, but very rarely. Still others use crutches, some are pushed in their wheelchairs by pals while others manoeuvre their electric chairs with great skill. There are those with heavy glasses, neck frames and sundry other contraptions. The overall impression, however, is of energy and dynamism; it is the noisy human throng, rushing in its own zig-zag, shuffling fashion to the dinner-table.

For me, however, memories of the CRC are indelibly marked by the tears and the chill in the marrow of the bones as we absorbed the news of Davoren's handicap, a vague indefinite prognosis on that first visit, but as the months and years went by, deeper and more searing realisations as almost all the stages of normal childhood development passed him by. Mostly, when the news was bad, we tried to be stoical (we knew we were not the only parents and children going through similar ordeals) or even seized on some straw of comfort or some strange quirk in our situation to make a joke and try to remain cheerful. But often we wept unashamedly and uncontrollably.

We also developed a routine of taking a detour to Dollymount beach on our way home to Drumcondra. On the beach there was space for our pain to cry out, to seep out. If it was not too cold, I would chase around with Dav on my shoulder, as we tried to over-compensate with giddy frolics. Brighid was much more inconsolable than I, for my years of spiritual and philosophical questing had rightly or wrongly made me stoical (on the surface at least). Still the sea would work some healing on us and we would eventually go home a little more composed for drinking our bitter cup. The pot of tea around our Bantry Road hearth would not exactly wipe all tears away, but it would balm the scoured and salty channels.

We had bought our house in Bantry Road just at the time when Davoren's handicap was confirmed. As we happily embraced our new home, we had no idea in our blessed innocence what a physical millstone it was to become for us. It would be hard to imagine a house more unsuitable for a handicapped child, with its many steps, small rooms and inadequate wiring. Yet buying the house had so completely drained our finances that for years we had no money to make the necessary adaptations.

□□□□

After the initial shock of our first CRC visit, we set about finding out as much as possible about Davoren's condition and learning all the practical things we could do to help him. We threw ourselves into physiotherapy routines (I even seriously considered trying to study physiotherapy) and tried all sorts of tricks and dodges to coax his muscles to respond appropriately. Our emphasis during those early years was on movement, on detecting and encouraging any signs of Davoren lifting himself or crawling, for example. Our hopes, how hopeless and forlorn they now seem, were that Davoren might eventually be able to stand or even walk in some fashion. We trained friends and baby-sitters to do exercises with him. Ingenious friends of ours constructed a slide and a sloping crawling hoist for Davoren (based on ideas we had seen in a book) to encourage co-ordinated crawling.

There were moments of giddy triumph as when Davoren raised himself on his arms as he lay stretched on his front on the physiotherapy ball (like a giant beach ball) or when, supported by one of us from behind, he high-stepped towards the other in a state of high elation. But in general the story of Davoren's first eight years was of him sliding back inexorably on the scale of physical co-ordination and development.

We met children and parents with whom we had started out on the same road, rolling and stretching on the gymnasium mats in the CRC when Davoren was a baby. Now their child was part of that gangly melee of children staggering along the corridors with the aid of a walking frame, or perhaps able with great effort to manipulate a wheelchair. To us these were feats of massive independence which we felt slipping away from Davoren.

These discrepancies were a feature of cerebral palsy as it had been explained to us; you could not predict at six months what degree of developmental breakdown would result. All we could see was that with Davoren the shake-out was much more cruel and comprehensive that we could have anticipated in our wildest imaginings.

In the meantime another aspect of Davoren's handicap, which was to exact a severe toll on us, had surfaced. During his first year he had his first epileptic seizure, resulting in an emergency rush to the Temple Street Hospital in the middle of the night. Thus began a sequence of crisis hospitalisations for Davoren, which occurred every four to six weeks during the worst years, and three or four times a year during his period of strongest health and maximum creativity from the age of nine to fifteen.

Even though Davoren's first bout of epilepsy was triggered by a high fever, it soon became apparent that this condition was a more deep-seated problem. In association with infections, he continued to have dramatic seizures which required swift medical intervention in the form of intravenous valium on a regular basis. But despite being put on anti-convulsant medication, Davoren also had many small seizures, dramatic and frightening to the uninitiated, from which he emerged spontaneously. It is a medical juggling act of considerable subtlety to prescribe a level of medication which keeps the seizures at bay sufficiently to prevent epilepsy taking over a person's life but not at too great a cost to their energy and alertness. It was a very significant factor in Davoren's life that he spent large chunks of his life fighting infection and on various medication (including antibiotics) which would deplete the reserves of any of us.

Also absolutely crucial to Davoren's sense of himself as it emerged in his poetry is that he was critically ill during several of these hospitalisations. At the age of about five or six Davoren was in a coma in Temple Street Hospital for about a week. Davoren's dramatic self-presentation — "Pain became my bed-fellow/ and despair my song./ God disappeared behind the clouds;/ I lost my star-signpost to hope" — was no rhetorical device.

I am infinitely grateful for all the care and treatment which Davoren received from nurses and doctors over the years — without the benefit of modern medicine, he would not have survived beyond babyhood — but there were dark moments. When Davoren was emerging from that coma in Temple Street to what we saw as his normal ebullient self, one senior doctor brought us out to the corridor and urged us to put him in an institution and forget about him.

Another regular incident which gave us a sharp stab was repeated so frequently that we eventually saw the funny side of it. Davoren's admissions usually took place at two or three in the morning and, when the initial crisis was over, a doctor would write up the file. All of the information was already in the hospital records but the complete medical history of this unusual case seemed to interest the young doctors who were invariably on duty. In a stupor we answered all the questions but the twist always came with the query: "And have you any other children?" This was a routine technical question, but always came at us with a huge emotional overload, such as the unspoken "apart from this helpless case with his catalogue of problems?"

The psychological strength of Davoren along with the normal resilience of children got him through those nightmare years. We marvelled at his robustness as time and time again he recovered well, but then after a few short weeks he would be struck down once more. The intervals of health were too short for us to have any secure base to chart a path for this bright but trapped child of ours.

A technical description of Davoren's handicaps presents a clinical picture of dis-order, dis-ease and dis-harmony which at a certain level was true of Davoren, but in a sense scarcely touches him at all. Davoren became known to most people through his words but my strong conviction, as a witness throughout his whole life, is that his pre-verbal presence in and through his various distortions was something powerful and mysterious in its own right. If I use words like grace and beauty and elegance about Davoren, they are not the besotted words of a grieving father. I could say the same about several friends of Davoren who are also speechless.

"To some it is given, to those that have eyes to see and ears to hear" — there is a lot of truth in this gnomic gospel saying about this quality of presence in Davoren. Without falling under the sway of any religious dogma, the only words that I can find to describe this phenomenon is that it is like a pure uncluttered manifestation of the human spirit. I was a constant witness to this dramatic, yet infinitely subtle, manifestation of Davoren's power on others; some people went straight to the heart with Davoren, shooting back his smiles or stares in reciprocation, while others were trapped in the tangles and contortions of Davoren's external appearance. I never did and still do not judge anyone on this matter because, to the core of my being, I was torn in two. With one eye (or 'I'), I saw or felt for most of the time this wonderful presence, but on other occasions I shared all the bafflement and pain of those who were frightened and struck dumb by the degree and extent of Davoren's handicaps.

□□□□

At the very early age of two, Davoren was provisionally assessed as mentally handicapped by the CRC. To us it seemed a very cursory assessment, with many of the questions asked being inappropriate, requiring Davoren to be able to physically respond in some way. Brighid in particular vigorously contested this assessment and we never allowed it to affect the way we engaged with him. We knew that the scale of Davoren's alertness was enormous, ranging from blankness to ecstasy, but we could not accept that the dance of merriment in his eyes in response to the repartee in the home or his rapt concentration on a piece of music indicated a mental retardation.

But with Davoren unable to utter a word or give any other clear physical responses, we, like him, were trapped. Davoren was transferred to the Special Care Unit of St Michael's House at Ballymun which he attended daily in between his hospital admissions and other crises. Brighid had in the meantime started part-time work with St Michael's House Training Centre in the same complex. Over the years she made a very original and valuable contribution in her work on personal development, relationships and sex education with teenagers and young adults.

With this double link to St Michael's, we were taken under the sheltering wing of this innovative organization. Brighid was a combative spirit in trying to overturn the assignment of Davoren to St Michael's House, but the three of us would never have survived those years without the resourceful and wide-ranging back-up from St Michael's.

In his 'Notes from a Bone Fragment' ("my parents homerically nurtured me with music, stories and moments of splendid madness") and in his poems, Davoren has very well described the atmosphere of hope and promise with which we tried to surround him in spite of his terrible handicaps. Of course Davoren's picture of our family life is too noble and rarified; nonetheless he captures something of the way in which Brighid's and my love of language and music sustained us during those years. By dint of his disability Davoren was willy-nilly locked into this family amalgam of despair, pain, faltering hopes and optimism against the odds.

Story-telling and games around the table were the most triumphant of these interludes of buoyancy. We had a very strikingly illustrated copy of *Goldilocks and the Three Bears* which we read regularly for Davoren. As time went on, various off-beat, irreverent and downright scabrous interpolations were introduced into the tale, but the significant link in recalling this episode was Davoren's ability to point to various items in the pictures. Sitting on Brighid's lap, he would stab at or nudge his little finger (it used to stick out from his folded fist) towards Papa Bear's pipe, Mama Bear's cup of tea or Baby Bear's glass of milk. (He also specialised in knocking objects like salt cellars, egg cups and plates off the table, which all contributed to the atmosphere of chaos in our household at the time.)

Davoren's "bony bottom" on his mother's thighs was his platform for lunging and twisting towards freedom and communication. I have a vivid picture of him contorting himself to lean back against Brighid's shoulder, kiss her and then look her in the eye with a mixture of pleading and power. Even yet I am puzzled that Brighid, with her background in remedial education, did not exploit earlier Davoren's mobility on her lap to work with letters or whatever. My only explanation is that the periods of remission from sickness, hospitalisation and stress were too brief and infrequent. Also we were still shell-shocked by the unfolding revelation of Davoren's handicaps, as each month further tightened the screws on his plight.

Meanwhile, I was the workhorse of the household, concentrating on trying to ease the stiffness from Davoren's limbs and to prevent deformities. As I rolled him on the floor, stretched him and massaged him, my hopes and dreams went far beyond these remedial measures. I clung for a very long time to innocent fantasies of Davoren making progress in mobility. During my teenage years sport was at the very heart of my enthusiasms; despite very modest ability, I tried my hand at everything, soccer, rugby, tennis and athletics. Thus I found it very hard to accept Davoren as being happy imprisoned as he was in immobility. In my day or night-time dreams, Davoren was, and still is, always walking or running.

Black Board, Red Letters, Gold Tears

As Davoren turned eight, several changes came together to mark a watershed in all our lives. First of all his health stabilised, the intervals between his hospitalisations became longer, his eating (liquidised food) improved somewhat and he generally became more robust. Secondly, after several years of anguished discussion and prayer, Brighid and I turned away with great sadness from the thought of having more children.

A crucial element in this decision was the result of a CAT-scan done on Davoren's brain in the old Richmond Hospital. This showed that Davoren's handicaps were not, or at least not primarily, the result of birth trauma or deprivation of oxygen as had been previously thought. The CAT-scan images showed agenesis of the corpus callosum, that is, a lack of development of the large structure joining the two hemispheres of the brain. The precise function of the corpus callosum is not very well understood, but at that stage the significance of the CAT-scan result was to increase the statistical chances of our having another handicapped child. At what was called a 'genetic counselling' session, we were given probabilities to conjure with, but the stark truth was that Brighid felt that the birth of another child with a disability would drive her over the edge altogether.

In order to cope with this gut-wrenching decision, Brighid decided to pursue a Master of Education course in Trinity College. This long-cherished goal of hers was now given greater impetus by her need to feel that she was making progress in some aspect of her life. In the very fibre of her being, Brighid felt that she had failed terribly. Because of her diabetes, she had assumed a burden of responsibility for Davoren's disability which was completely unwarranted and which in my heart of hearts I never laid on her. I can truly say that to my recollection I never

31

said anything to her to suggest that I was not proud of her for having borne our son.

While Brighid and I were polemicists against the rigidities of male and female stereotypes, it is fair to say that at that stage we were acting out our response to Davoren's implosion into our lives in deeply contrasting ways. Brighid was dramatic and expressive, very strongly giving the impression of being on the verge of cracking up under the strain. In the dark of the night, in the quiet of our bedroom, after the umpteenth time getting up to attend to Davoren's distress, she shrieked and railed against God, whom she professed not to believe in any more. She experienced each hospitalisation as a sword piercing her; after the initial crisis was over, she often found it extremely hard to go back and visit Davoren; then once she visited him, she found it almost impossible to tear herself away from his helpless position in a hospital cot with needles stuck in his arm. The acute contrast with most of the other children, recovering from 'normal' illnesses, was too much for her to bear.

I was outwardly more calm and accepting — I coped better with the medical crises (Brighid had rebelled against the nursing background of both her parents and her brother and sister). But I too had huge bottled-up feelings of failure and disappointment which I only gradually sorted out as Davoren grew older.

Thus Brighid's decision to go back studying was immensely liberating. Despite the pressure of essays and assignments, she enjoyed the renewed intellectual challenge and made new friends, particularly during the first year of the course. She was much happier and more relaxed with Davoren now that he wasn't the sole focus of her life and, as a result, her creativity with him flowered in new ways. These fresh initiatives, which drew her into a more intense bond with Davoren, kicked back hard at her as she moved into the second stage of the M.Ed with the requirement to research and write a thesis.

The third change impacting on Davoren was our decision to let go of our efforts to improve Davoren's mobility and concentrate on his chances of communicating clearly. Because Brighid had a highly visible public role in typing with Davoren and with advocating his cause, she always liked to give me credit when the occasion demanded. And on the matter of charting this new communication voyage for Davoren, she was right. My heart had been set on seeing Davoren move, but, in a moment of lucidity, I had seen that our energy reserves were limited and that if we tried to work with Davoren on all fronts, we would achieve nothing and wear ourselves out completely.

I was sure of the brightness of his responses and felt confident that we could make some progress in drawing on that intelligence within. So I started visiting the Speech Therapy Unit in the CRC with Davoren and liaising with the workers in the St Michael's House Developmental Day Centre (formerly the Special Care Unit). Since I was working evenings and nights, I was free to follow up these contacts during the day while Brighid was at Trinity. The approach with the therapists ranged from trying to get Davoren to point at pictures to jiggling around with switches that he might operate.

Davoren's ability to do what we asked of him was frustratingly erratic. We placed wedges and cushions on his chair and tried all sorts of manoeuvres to get him into a position of stable control. Despite all these efforts, his chair seemed more and more like a prison locking him into inertia and impotence. What Davoren thought of all this baby work with pictures and switches, while his mother as an impresario of communication and her lap as a platform for his self-expression lay in waiting behind the scenes, I can only guess.

In the autumn and early winter of 1982, the dining-room table ritual of knocking objects onto the floor and pointing to pictures in books began to turn into formal lessons on matching concrete and abstract shapes, matching of coloured objects and working with numbers. Another very important pre-communication episode involved a musical toy with the scale arranged in a circle with big coloured buttons. Davoren became particularly animated as Brighid banged out all the old favourite tunes on this simple toy and he would then follow the sequence. Davoren's whole technique of using Brighid's lap as a springboard for his diving and falling onto objects was perfected using this musical toy. It was this kind of excitation in Davoren which convinced us that we were on the right track.

The next link in the communication chain was provided by a metal blackboard with magnetic plastic letters in bright colours. Brighid started teaching him his alphabet using the plastic letters. The 'lessons' turned into a game again as, in order to indicate his recognition of a letter, Davoren improvised a method of knocking off the letters he didn't want by sweeping his fist across the blackboard.

> That word 'Mama' fumblingly pushed with folded fist across the black meadow of magnetic board liberated me from an eternity of nothingness. Bright red was the word, bright gold were the tears of relief in my heart! My jubilation lit the skies.

This is Davoren's recollection of his breakthrough which he wrote in 1989 in his autobiographical introduction to his book of poems. My own memory of the details of those dramatic weeks early in 1983 is now hazy and in any case I probably missed some of the crucial moments, working as I did at night. Fortunately Brighid recorded the whole sequence, moment by painstaking moment, in a series of notebooks and scrapbooks. Her own note on Davoren's jubilation says he "got so excited, he nearly went through the ceiling."

Later she describes his first spelling out of his own name. Davoren's task was to move the letters from the top right-hand corner of the board, where they were jumbled, down to the bottom left-hand corner where Brighid had written his name in chalk:

> Davoren 'cycled' with legs over to direction of duster in box — seemed to want me to rub out chalked letters DAVOREN (as if he didn't want them). Then got excited and began task of 'writing' letters. Pulled each letter down and had no errors. Time: 45 minutes. Comment: seems to have wanted to show he could spell it out himself.

Brighid then goes on to record how Davoren built up the word DADA from the combined jumbled letters for MAMA and DAVOREN without her having shown him the word written in chalk. Her comment was: "built DADA aurally: find this hard to fathom."

She really began to unlock his mind when she taught him 'yes' and 'no'. His answers to various questions, large (are you happy? are you clever?) and small (do you need to be changed? would you like chocolate?) could be indicated by pointing to the bold-coloured 'yes' and 'no'. Brighid notes: "Pointing involves shifting weight from side to side using cycling movement and touching with hand." On the pivot of his "bony bottom", Davoren was launched into a new world.

◻◻◻◻

Shortly after the blackboard triumph, Brighid transferred him to the typewriter. He caught on to finding the letters very rapidly and appreciated enormously seeing the results of his work on the page. Brighid commented: "Puts little finger on letter, but often slides fist along several before stopping at letter. Top row difficult to get. If arm 'spastic,' I don't attempt. The typewriter was Catherine's (a helper at the time) idea; I thought at first letters too small."

One or two of the helpers and I coached him with words and practised pointing at the letters. Monica Gorman was an AnCo trainee on placement with us from St Michael's House at the time. A small, stocky, vibrant Dublin girl with a shock of red (or at various times more garishly coloured) hair, Monica was big-hearted with a strong voice and a wide range of sporting, political and intellectual interests. She and Davoren had a spirited knockabout relationship and under Brighid's tutelage Monica immersed herself in the communication work. The sight of Davoren and Monica battling at the keyboard with much jostling and shouting was quite a spectacle; she would try to peer round him to see what letter he was trying to reach while he would be nudging back against her for a kiss. His poem about her written after she had completed her placement and had returned on a visit captures her wholehearted defiant optimism: "Cypress tree persuading/ questioning sapling/ not to despair of acquiring maturity;/ loving sap seeping through woody apertures,/ what I do issues from a faith in me."

"I like a lisl kes please," he typed with Brighid on 20th April 1983 at a stage when his writing vocabulary was very limited and he was having a stab at spelling phonetically whatever he wanted to say. Another day he typed, "jumpey tojerdo please", which Brighid interpreted as "jumpy together", a request for a "horsey", a kind of game we played with him straddled across my leg while I imitated a horse's gallop. One of his favourite ploys in introducing himself was: "I am a clever boy." Needy childishness alternated with brash precocity as Davoren emerged from his shell of silence. Even the words he used for Brighid and myself, 'Mama' and 'Dada,' betrayed this ambivalence. Our son, whom we had spent so many hours cradling in his helplessness, nestling on our laps (very often the only way to successfully get food into him was to lock his spastic body into the hollow between our legs), was finding a voice — the simplest declaration seemed like a revelation.

Brighid's first notebook is full of references to friends and visitors to the house nudging close to Davoren as he sat at the keyboard. He would reach out to touch and be touched by them and would then turn towards the keyboard and type out their names and some simple phrase such as "I love you" or "I like Angela". Angela Boushel had come to the house as a young teenager when Davoren was less than a year-old, offering to take him for walks. She had become a great friend of the family and after Brighid's death, despite being in exile in Scotland, remained the senior and most respected of the 'siblings'. All his life, Davoren was one of the most loved, hugged and touched people in the universe; he never lost his delight in, nor his need for the reassurance of warm physical contact, but this new 'simple' act of naming his loved ones gave him power and independence.

Moods of a darker hue also intruded. Out of the blue on 22nd March 1983, he typed for Brighid: "I am sad." This occurred at a time when he had been taught very few words. Brighid noted: "I had been talking to him ten minutes earlier about how I felt. I had said I felt sad, fed up, depressed. I had been crying. I didn't say why I had been sad. He must have felt my sadness or was sad himself. I asked him to repeat the word he had just typed as I couldn't believe what he'd typed. He repeated 'sad'." After further exchanges during which she checked out his message, she noted: "I told him he had made me happy again and he got very excited."

Reality encroached in another way the following day when he was hospitalised and stayed away from home for two-and-a-half weeks altogether as he went for recuperation to Glenanaar, a hostel run by St Michael's House. The conversation (so to speak) resumed on 10th April when he typed: "Are you like me?" We then had a long conversation with him about what he meant. Brighid noted: "When we were explaining the difference between us in terms of handicap, I got tearful and he indicated that he wanted to type more." He asked: "Are you sad?" Brighid continued: "We explained that we were happy, but sometimes sad. He got very excited when we told him he made us happy because he was clever and because he was Davoren."

But even more sombre was the fact that Davoren's breakthrough provoked not only jubilation and celebration but also consternation. Staff at the Central Remedial Clinic and at St Michael's House could not easily accept that this child whom they generally saw locked in inertia could generate these sentences. They saw and could appreciate his transformation on Brighid's lap when she made a visit to either centre but were non-committal at best about his new-found intelligence. Strangely, those who worked most closely with Davoren on a day-to-day basis found it easier to delight in and accept his new status. It was those who saw him for brief periods in assessment mode who proved most obstructive.

Brighid's notebooks record an early 'test' where she typed with Davoren with a blindfold over her eyes. Looking back on this period, I am amazed at Brighid's consenting to submit herself and Davoren to such humiliating experiences. The so-called tests did not go well. The simple explanation for this is that working with Davoren involved fine-tuning both on the part of Davoren and of the helper. If Davoren was in a high state of spasticity, there was very little you could do with him. If he was tense or untrusting with the person he was working with, nothing would happen. The best illustration of this was that only some of the helpers ever learned to type with Davoren. Several of them, who had an excellent relationship with him, could never trust themselves enough to go with the combination of jagged and subtle movements by which he indicated his letters. My own severe trials in communicating with Davoren, which I will outline more fully later, constitute a story shot through with grief, doubt, obstinacy and perversity.

A certain wilfulness in Davoren also played a part in these test failures. "When those who doubt the authenticity of my voice ask how can a boy like that possibly communicate with such severe physical handicap, a satanic fury overcomes me," he wrote in the introduction to *Not Common Speech*. We are looking back at the very early days of Davoren's communication but I have no doubt that already he was stubbornly furious at being tested, at being "turned on the relentless roasting spit of logic".

Davoren also wrote: "In their rational mood, they (my parents) too engaged in doubting-Thomas fact-searching before they fully believed I was intellectually unimpaired."

Looking back after all these years, I am amazed at how probing and questioning Brighid was. The notebooks are full of references to her checking and rechecking the phrases he came out with, interrogating him and herself about where he picked up unusual words, about how he managed to spell certain words correctly while in other cases he would come up with the most outlandish phonetic experiments.

❏❏❏❏

On 20th May 1983, he typed with Brighid: "You are the arcqetip parents." Brighid notes that earlier in the day she and I had been clowning around with Davoren, saying silly things to him such as "We're a mad pair to have for parents. But would you swop us?" Brighid now asked him to repeat the sentence, which he did, and then asked him to explain it.

"You are the best parents I cood have."

"Where did you hear this big word?"

"From a sentese I herd Dada say aqwileago."

"Do you know many big words like that?"

"Yes. I no a lot of words."

Strange as it may seem, 'archetype' is a word that I would use a lot, based on my background in philosophy, I suppose, but I would also pepper it into everyday conversations as a kind of joke or code. Another linguistic

tic of mine that Davoren picked up and played with later on was my use of the word 'actually' or 'aktually' as he spelt it at first.

He was on a roll that evening but it ended on a downbeat note when I took over trying to type with him and he typed "I am sick a..." before he slumped, unable to continue. It transpired that he was merely extremely constipated and we had to give him a suppository. In fact Davoren often had to break off from the most interesting or playful chats for some such severe discomfort.

The following day Brighid had to embark on an intensive bout of detective work that would increasingly preoccupy her as Davoren's vocabulary outstripped his ability to spell. Starting off with me he typed: "Wat is lazy av?" We both got discouraged with our slow progress so with Brighid he then typed: "Wat is lazraverwil?" When Brighid asked him where he heard the word, he replied: "On the wefer forecast." Brighid went through all the possibilities which his attempted phonetic spelling suggested like 'occasional,' 'isolated,' 'light to moderate' and 'light drizzle' until finally hitting on the correct one, 'light or variable'.

But the conversation did not always involve ferreting around for unusual words. "Fukan tipriter," he wrote as his fingers jammed once again in the keys. Thus began a series of inventive spellings of the F-word, ranging from "afukof and shut up", and "aw faqof" to "awfaqwit". This gave him an outlet for the feelings of frustration and confinement he often felt from being locked into this close bond with Brighid in order to find his voice. There were times when the intensity of these two strong characters locked in combat was too much for me.

Another important feature of his development was that Davoren was not taught to read in any conventional sense and his ability to read as he progressed was greatly hampered by his poor head and eye control. He could not scan a page, his head would fall or get twisted away from the page or he would otherwise get locked into a spasm. The best posture for reading was to take him on your lap and hold him over the page. Since my periods of typing with him were already becoming short and erratic, I often took on the task of reading aloud to him as he pushed and shoved and cycled on my lap.

Little Sound, Strong Will, Hot Tears

A series of deeper questions surfaced around May and June 1983, six months or so after Davoren began communicating. It was sparked off by Brighid's contact with her thesis supervisor in Trinity College, Professor Dan Murphy. Dan's lectures on the philosophy of education and on the Jewish philosopher Martin Buber in particular had stimulated her enormously. On Saturday afternoon 4th June, a conversation was started with Monica about a trip Brighid and Davoren had made the previous day to Trinity College. "When we arived in the car, I was xcited an Mama was nervous," he started. Later with Brighid he gave his explanation. "Becos everybody was loking at us." He continued: "It azdaz me when everybody dos stare at me becos I am not a faking ixsibshen." Brighid interrogated him to discover that 'azdaz' meant 'upsets' and 'ixsibshen' 'exhibition'. There followed a long consoling session with Brighid leading on to Davoren's lengthy meal-time. When the conversation resumed in the evening, Davoren said he was glad to have met Dan and then added: "How will Dan answer me?" Brighid was puzzled by this and asked Davoren what question did he have for Dan to answer. "How dos God like a child like me?" (It is important to bear in mind that the above conversation was spread out over eight hours.)

Davoren's spiritual question seemed to be based on an imaginary conversation he'd had with Dan and on something he picked up from the meeting, as God hadn't figured in the conversation between Dan and Brighid or during the brief period Dan and Davoren were alone together.

A few days later, on Thursday 9th June, Davoren asked Catherine O'Reilly, one of his helpers at the time, if she questioned about God when she was a little girl. He then asked her: "Are you a relejyus person?"

Brighid then asked him whom he knew who was religious. He answered Dan, then Jack, and finally Brighid which he spelt as 'Brid' at the time. Brighid was probably taken aback by this as she wouldn't have counted herself as high on the religious scale so she asked him what he meant by religious. "I meen poetik," he replied. After Brighid said nothing, he continued: "I love how poetry gets to the hart." I must have been at home that night as Brighid records that the evening was rounded off with me reading some poetry to him.

The following day after a conversation with Brighid about physical and mental handicaps, he typed: "What dos Dan think abat fizzakly handicappt poets?" When Brighid asked him who was a physically handicapped poet, he replied: "I am." He then indicated that he had a poem in his head. When Brighid asked him would he write it down soon, he indicated "no". When asked when he would write it down, he replied: "When I seditsfed wis it" (when I'm satisfied with it).

Brighid's record for the next day was as follows:

> He was in very subdued form today and I didn't ask him any questions. He typed spontaneously: "I am sad today." I asked why. "I am a lissl handicappt boy a no good for any thing person." I was upset on reading the above. "Are you weeping becos I sed what I am xpeerensing akutly al the time?" I talked to him for a while about how I felt.

Sunday morning started off with a difficult session with me. "Ktarez" was the best I could make of his first effort at a word. When asked did he want to type more, Davoren indicated 'Yes'. We continued and, by dint of great determination on Davoren's part, we managed: "I am a qwestion se..." While the word 'qwestion' was very clear, each letter had been a struggle and I got tired and disheartened and gave up.

Brighid and I were both a bit fed up with the difficulties which I was experiencing typing with him but the gloom was dispersed by an afternoon visit from an old friend of Brighid's, Mari Fitzduff, now living near the shore of Lough Neagh in Co Tyrone. Davoren started off his chat with Mari with his usual lovey-dovey stuff, touching her and typing her name but he later typed: "Sorry I am feeling fuken ofel today." Brighid ascertained that the reason for his bad humour was the earlier strain over his typing efforts with me.

At about ten o'clock that night, Brighid got back to working with him and gradually teased out of him that he had been trying to start a poem with me in the morning. I reprint it exactly as it emerged on that summer's evening in 1983. At this stage, we were using capitals all the time for Davoren's typing.

KESAW

I AM A QWESTYON, STIFF XAM,
TEST ME WHEN IL B REDHY,
EHKAPING WHER POETRY GOES AWHILE,
PUTING RISULTS BEHIND ME.

The only really difficult word to decipher was the title of the poem which Brighid guessed as 'Keepsake' from previous experience of him using 'z' for 'ps'. When Brighid asked him what a keepsake was, he answered: "somthing you want to giv to sombody as a gift". He claimed he had heard Dan Murphy use the word in connection with a copy of Rodin's statue 'The Kiss' which would have been on his desk during the visit to his rooms in Trinity. Davoren said he wanted to give the poem to me as a keepsake. The edited version of the poem which Brighid included in a handwritten book of his first eighty poems reads:

Keepsake: for Dada

I am a question, stiff exam,
Test me when I'll be ready,
Escaping where poetry goes awhile,
Putting results behind me.

This may not count for much as poetry, but as a succinct statement of the dilemma and hopes facing Davoren at the time it was incomparable. Brighid's own commentary in the handwritten volume sums it up accurately:

Davoren's first poem, written in June 1983, was a statement by him of his own autonomy and puzzling uniqueness, resistant to psychological testing. He had just been made aware of the results of a test which was sceptical of his intelligence. He claimed to find respite in poetry from the injustice of such testing.

The after-shock of the poem reverberated over the next few days. While Brighid's notes show her delight and amazement at his poem, they also show a certain gloom and consternation. I think she realised that Davoren was raising the stakes, that the whole issue of his and her credibility would loom larger as he began to make more outlandish claims and that she was in danger of being sucked into the vortex of Davoren's battles.

On Tuesday, he asked her, "Hav I got ryting gifts?" to which she replied that she thought he had, to judge by his poem. She then asked him what he would like to be when he grew up. He paused for a while, then typed: "A man, a ryter, a clever persen, a good frend."

The following day, working with me, he was very animated and giddy and came out with the sentence: "I am a riter and a poet." The conversation had to be broken off at that point for a stressful visit to the CRC and wasn't resumed again until the following Sunday when he asked me: "Are you a poet?" Brighid records that I said "yes" and that he then finished off with "I love poetry".

❑❑❑❑

The whole attitude in the house towards poetry, and indeed towards Davoren's poems in particular, was considerably more complex than is accounted for in Davoren's passion for his new-found path to liberation. Brighid was the true uncomplicated poetry-lover among us. In her relatively short and stressful life, poetry was an abiding source of nourishment to her. Starting with her studies in UCD, she liked Chaucer, the Metaphysical poets, TS Eliot and Yeats among others; she also fell under the spell of Paddy Kavanagh. But she continued her explorations, uncovering new treasures like Osip Mandelstam, Anna Akhmatova, ee cummings, Sylvia Plath and Denise Levertov, to name but a few. Long before Seamus Heaney became a household name to conjure with, she read and appreciated his work. She genuinely believed in the power of literature, and poetry in particular, to open up new horizons in the young. If she had a faith, it was a poetic type of faith. But there was no admixture of personal striving, competitiveness or narcissism in Brighid's love of poetry; she had no desire to join the pantheon. Her use of language was sensitive, quick-witted, quirky and racy but she had no pretensions to write poetry. She could turn her hand to amusing, risqué doggerel or produce a witty limerick for a special occasion but her real forte was cartoons and her writing tended to have some of that lampooning cartoon character.

One of Brighid's favourite satiric targets was my tortured love-affair with Dame Philosophy; in her own pithy way she captured the essence of my fascination, yet in the end, dissatisfaction with philosophy. Philosophy was my first adult love, but it ended up being an unrequited passion in that my wanting to embrace all the questions at once tended to smother the ordered harmony of a sustained relationship. Poetry kept leaking out the sides. Like many other young people, my first poems were swooning expressions of love for some real dame, having been let down by Dame Philosophy. Poetry continued to play a part in my life over many years, but I was very timid about any talent that I might have had and never took it very seriously. I felt very unsure about standards in poetry. I was suspicious of poetry's charm and guile. Sometimes I thought I could tell the gold from the dross; at other times, I felt rudderless. Also, unlike Brighid, I read poetry very intermittently. I seemed to have no stamina for reading poetry on a regular basis. It was Brighid who would introduce me to new writers, and it was in reading aloud for Davoren that my love for poetry kept being rekindled.

I unfortunately brought some of these ambivalent feelings about poetry into play in my reactions to Davoren's espousing of poetry as his medium of expression. His hero-worship of me (later on he would have plenty of opportunity to redress the balance in contemplating my feet of clay) set off all my hesitations, doubts and fears about poetry. It is embarrassing and faintly ridiculous to reveal these reactions to the clumsily-typed expressions of a mute eight-year-old child, but it is a mark of the deadly seriousness with which we took his words and postures of defiance. In the midst of our jubilation, both Brighid and I were aware of the emergence of something uncanny and unsettling in Davoren. It was as if he had discovered a mission in the midst of his appalling handicaps. Where all the external assessors of Davoren missed out was in not having this deep experience of Davoren all fired up and determined to make his mark. There was steel in him despite his childishness and frailty.

There was an extra edge to my reservations about Davoren's poetry in that it seemed like a well-trodden path for young handicapped Dubliners. I used to joke with him: "Oh no, not another poet, why couldn't you be a scientist or something?" Davoren in contrast seemed to relish following in the footsteps of Christy Brown and Christopher Nolan. It was important to him to have his handicapped heroes.

◻◻◻◻

As if to illustrate the saying of Brendan Behan, "'Twas far from *angst* that you were reared", Davoren went off on another tack entirely for a few weeks after his first poem. It happened with a visit from Barbara Callan, a great friend from our earliest days together. Barbara, living in Connemara with her husband Dave Hogan, was expecting their first child and her pregnancy prompted Davoren into a full-scale exploration of his own origins. This turned into a fairly comic exploration of sex (the sexual curiosity of young boys was almost Brighid's 'Mastermind' special subject) and of the nature of his disability (a much more searing subject altogether). Brighid and I were away for a few days' break after which he resumed his 'rattlebag' of questions — about God, death and the after-life (all subjects as calculated to arouse as much discomfort in Brighid as his talk of poetry did in me). He claimed to remember when he was born and the time that he spent in the incubator in Holles Street.

He was working quite well with Monica, offering comments about the pats on the head and the 'God help us' attitudes which he often encountered when out for walks. But with me he had come to a full-stop. Both Brighid and I were exasperated by this impasse. She alternated between blaming me for my lack of trust (checking and re-checking what letter he was indicating) and berating Davoren for too readily getting discouraged. There was nervousness and impatience on both sides. Davoren's response to this frustration was a savage attack on the sceptical, perfectionist aspect of my personality. He prefaced the poem with a question: "Is Dada geten down about me communkating wis him?" The poem then followed:

A LITTEL SOUND

CAN YOU XCAVAT MY VERY XSISTENS
LIKE A MOUND,
DIGGING LUCK, JETTISONING CHANS
TO THE GROUND?
YOU MAK LYF XACTING,
PAY DEN WIS HOT TEERFULNES,
JACK, HAV PASHENS WIS MY LITTEL SOUND.

Leading on to the corrected version:

A Little Sound

Can you excavate my very existence
 like a mound,
Digging luck, jettisoning chance
 to the ground?
You make life exacting —
pay then with hot tearfulness—
Jack, have patience with my little sound.

When Brighid pointed out that I might be upset on reading the poem, he softened the blow by typing: "You are my best frend and fader and I love you very muc." Two days later he asked, "Are you sedisfed wis the produsyon?" and afterwards added the comment: "I want somday to be as good a poet as Dada."

Trying to plot the sequence of Davoren's language development is a labyrinthine exercise, sometimes revealing, often amusing but often also plain puzzling. Some inconsistencies are explained by the fact that Brighid would often guess a word half-way through in order to speed up the process. This would lead to some words being spelt correctly which Davoren wouldn't have encountered in written form before. But Brighid's notes also show many occasions where she made mistakes in anticipating what he was trying to say. The pages are full of cross-outs (she taught Davoren early on to use the cross-out key on the typewriter), false starts and battles by him to express what he wanted to say as opposed to what she thought he might want to put down. From now on, however, I will only very occasionally include Davoren's misspellings and the original versions of poems and comments.

Brighid's notes also chart her explorations of how he discovered some unusual words. Davoren often gave cryptic or misleading accounts himself of where he heard words; favoured explanations were that he heard it on BBC Radio Three or that I had used it. When Brighid was asked about this in interviews, she often repeated these explanations so that they then became the legend behind which there was only a certain amount of truth. It was true that Brighid listened to Radio Three a lot and when Davoren's unusual turns of phrases, questionings and oracular pronouncements began to emerge, we became more aware of the unusual conversations to which he had been a captive listener over the years.

The truth is that, like all language acquisition especially that in early childhood, there was an elusive or fathomless heart to Davoren's emergence as a language-being. The long years of his silence were an extreme of human experience and the years of his 'uncommon speech' were strange and perplexing to a corresponding degree.

◻◻◻◻

The surreal juxtaposition of metaphysical flights of fancy and the inexorable toll his handicap took on him is well-illustrated by an episode during these early days of his writing. When Shay Caffrey, a psychologist and work colleague of Brighid's, called, Davoren started to type a sentence for him. In line with his distrust of psychologists and their assessments of him to date, he typed: "I am pleased to say he is no psychologist." But this short sentence was broken off for two hours while Davoren recovered from a *petit mal* epileptic seizure. Later that day a friend from Sri Lanka, Lakshme, called with her little daughter, Asshi. During a provocative conversation about God and the differences between men and women and Eastern and Western approaches, Davoren came out with this sentence: "Since there is utter perfection in heaven, the handicap is easier to bear in the present life."

Brighid had a caustic line on heaven, miracles and all that side of spirituality (one of her favourite challenges was "Let's see an amputated limb replaced") and so she oscillated between affirming his expressions of consoling faith and taking him on. Her mood was not sweetened when Davoren came out with sentences like: "Question what values you follow."

Another fruitful activity of his at the time was drawing. This may seem a surprising claim in view of my previous descriptions of his gross motor handicap and overall difficulties, but we are talking about a period when Davoren was at the peak of his powers. At a time of the day when his energy was high, and if his muscle tone was reasonably relaxed, he would fall to one side in his chair and with a marker attached to his hand make ferocious arcs in an effort to produce his drawing. It was one of the few activities which he could sometimes manage in his chair.

Brighid's notebooks contain several of these drawings to which he would give typically provocative titles. 'Death Drowning,' 'Australia — a kangaroo, cats and dogs swimming in the sea' and 'Trouble Holiday' are among notebook entries. A particularly strong drawing in the middle of August was called 'Mama and Dada on Holiday'. It seemed to refer to a joking conversation earlier that morning when he had said to us: "Mind you behave yourselves on holiday." We were leaving for Donegal while Davoren was going to stay with a young couple under a St Michael's House 'Breakaway' scheme. Brighid records him being very giddy altogether during this episode. A conversation the previous day had started with an enquiry about where his boldness came from, leading on to more probings about sex. He had concluded that the whole business of women and men and children was a catastrophe. After some puzzlement, Brighid noted that the phrase probably went back to a story I used to tell from the novel *Zorba the Greek* by Kazanzakis. The cerebral, reflective Englishman asks the elemental Zorba if he is married. "What," Zorba replies, "am I not a man? Of course I am married — wife, house, children — the whole catastrophe."

His next poem reverted to his anger at people who undermined his intelligence.

Nothingness

Are you upset when
wounds no sooner heal
than open to reveal
a deeper darkness?
To know for certain I exist,
I encounter loneliness and fear.

Both Brighid and Davoren were fired up after the holidays and a further poem followed a few days later, one which further tightened the screws on our sense of incredulity about the precocity of his thoughts.

A Burden Shared

Theoretically taken we delight in our privacy,
Loneliness, punishing memories assuaged.
Vacant as cadavers, cavernous we lie.
Philosophy is only pain and darkness;
poetry, music, beauty vaporize and die.
Religion questions death and life;
experimenting with panaceas gains no territory
— only God our prayer prescribes.

Brighid's note to this poem in the handwritten book of his early poems (transcribed much later) gave a relatively calm, measured reaction. She wrote: "This poem took a long time and a lot of effort to do (three days). Davoren was very worked up while doing it. It seems to be an attack on our values and an attempt to remind us of the supremacy of religion. He was asking many questions at the time of writing concerning the reasons for his handicap." The scrapbook, containing the original work-sheets for the poem, tells of a much more disturbed reaction. She was shocked at the authority with which he purported to speak, irritated at his bumptious tone and disconcerted at the possibility that the whole enterprise was getting out of hand. "Halfway through the poem, I had an awful feeling that he might be a reincarnation! I said, 'Is this you doing the poem?' He indicated 'No'. I said, 'Who?' He answered 'Me' and giggled and then typed: 'I was messing. Sorry, Mama.'" A sense of disquiet remained with her for several weeks which Davoren dispelled in his own inimitable fashion.

While the images in the line "vacant as cadavers, cavernous we lie" cannot but make an impact, I also reacted rather negatively to the poem as a poem, considering it inelegant and preachy. But the most dramatic aftermath was a no-holds-barred debate he had with a friend of ours, Íde Ní Laoghaire, who was living with us at the time. Íde, an acute mind with a training in philosophy, challenged him on his sweeping generalisations, treating him as an intellectual equal. Brighid recorded that it was late in the evening and Davoren was very tired but determined to take up the cudgels. However, his first typed statement was defensive and evasive: "I experience intense irritation when a banal statement is made." Things went from bad to worse when Íde continued to be robust in demanding to know what he meant by his castigation of music, poetry and beauty. Davoren got abusive, calling her silly, telling her to piss off and accusing her of nattering and destroying "a great exchange of critical analysis". There was fire in both their bellies at this stage as Davoren was grunting, straining, lunging, twisting and thrashing about in a demented fashion towards the end: angry, fiery and upset. He eventually apologised for calling her silly and a reconciliation of sorts was arrived at. I think Brighid hit the nail on the head in her notes, where she commended Íde for taking him on as an equal but noted that as Davoren "was emotionally only eight, he thus fared badly in the ensuing dialogue."

❐ ❐ ❐ ❐

During that night he got sick with a high fever and convulsions and ended up in Temple Street Hospital, where he was kept in for a week. Hospital was generally a miserable time for Davoren in that even when the immediate crisis was over, he was often stuck in bed with little or no stimulation. His condition was also often the subject of much staring and bafflement from the other sick children. This time however there was a difference. He insisted upon a note being pinned to the end of his bed saying, "I like being treated as potentially intelligent." One of the younger doctors on his rounds noticed Davoren's sign and engaged him in chat, to which Davoren responded: "He exonerated the medical profession."

The campaigning side of Davoren emerged with his assertion that "I want people to know about handicapped children's appalling treatment." There was a cruel downside to Davoren's zeal on this occasion as he and Brighid became concerned about another young handicapped child in a nearby bed. He was very frail and rigidly spastic like Davoren. He was crying a lot and didn't seem very responsive. Davoren was in the habit of making crowing noises in response to the crying. Brighid's heart went out to this other unstimulated, helpless creature on whom the other 'normal' children in the ward also gazed with fright so she asked Davoren for his opinion. He said: "He is not very clever." Mother and son then shared a deep sadness for a few moments as both realised that Davoren's own lack of response and pitiful crying often evoked this very same reaction from onlookers.

Brighid's exhausting efforts at the typewriter in the hospital, using pillows and all sorts of makeshift arrangements, were rewarded with his first poem addressed to her, a poem which was also his response to her annoyance and disquiet at his previous declamatory poem:

Cantata (for Mama)

Have I exactly illuminated your lantern,
banishing almost all black fear?
Backlogs of sacrifice, blind love,
vanquish false mavericks.

Brighid commented: "The poem is connected with 'Burden Shared' as I had reacted somewhat negatively to that poem, fearing that the poem was something outside of him. I had been more and more convinced of late of his gifts and he knows this, yet a vestige of questioning remains as to how come he's so intelligent. This is, I think, the reference to '*almost all* black fear'. Line 3 is a tribute to my working with him (despite the ambiguities in my mind about my 'blind' love)." When she questioned him the following day about what "black fear" related to, he replied, "Fear for my intelligence, just fear that nobody will believe in me." Davoren claimed 'Cantata' as one of his favourite poems. He explained that he had cynics in mind under the heading of 'mavericks'. Brighid wrote elsewhere: "It is a reassurance of love conquering doubt." The title of the poem was particularly appropriate because at that stage in Brighid's life one of her major consolations at such a bleak time of the year was a series of Bach Cantatas conducted by John Beckett which were held in St Ann's Church in Dawson Street every year in early spring.

There was a rush of energy and creativity when Davoren was discharged from hospital. He always seemed to find a new sense of enchantment being with us and with his friends in his own home after a serious illness. This delight did not, however, translate into a greater spirit of co-operation. We borrowed a video recorder from St Michael's House to make a film of his method of working. It proved very difficult to capture him vividly on tape but when we eventually got him into lively and supple condition, we asked him to type a simple sentence to illustrate his abilities. He typed: "I identify wis qwestyons about wimen who are carying babees." He followed this up with: "We are actisipating long awated verificashyon and recnishyon of our grativity."

He frequently tormented Brighid with mischievous stories which led her on wild goose chases checking out his inventions. She would get angry and frustrated with him. Then there would be a big reconciliation scene with promises made that he wouldn't indulge in fiction again. We eventually realised that it was Davoren's way of testing limits in the absence of opportunities for 'conventional' rebellious behaviour — and a very effective and perilous way it was: effective in that it provoked dramatic outbursts from Brighid and perilous in that it made the job of convincing the sceptics about Davoren's talents doubly difficult. (With the passage of time, I think I understand much better the 'perverse reasoning' whereby Davoren often seemed to spike his own best interests by messing up tests and inventing fictions.)

Babies, sex and death continued to be major preoccupations in his chats; these themes came together unhappily in a poem he wrote concerning the birth of a very severely handicapped child to friends of ours. Baby Laura had Edward's Syndrome which is associated with a very short life expectancy. She was in intensive care in Holles Street at the time Davoren wrote the poem and died some months after going home with her parents. Brighid and I had been talking about the difficulty of finding an appropriate way to acknowledge Laura's birth.

Cot, Pyrrhic Only

No excitement or congratulations
which acclaim most felicitous arrivals.
Frequent expressions of regretfulness
must produce turbulence or pain.

□□□□

If Brighid was tormented during this period by Davoren's continuing antics, it is fair to say that I was tortured and at my wit's end. Davoren and I seemed to get locked into anxiety and uncertainty every time we sat down in front of the typewriter. This problem never left us but a decisive change in my attitude occurred on the evening of the Stephen Hawking programme described in the first chapter.

The Hawking-inspired burst of creativity has always stood out for me as a turning-point in my struggles with Davoren, but I only now fully understand the reason why as I re-read Brighid's notes twelve years later. The account which I wrote in the first chapter of Davoren's reaction to hearing Stephen Hawking was wrong in several important respects (It was written without consulting any notes as I feared that I would never start this memoir of Davoren if I began burrowing into the archives). First, Davoren's jumping on my lap had been so startling and energetic that I had felt inspired to sit with him at the typewriter myself, even though I would normally have ceded to Brighid when he was exhibiting such urgency to communicate.

Of course it was still a slow and halting struggle compared to Brighid's method of working with him (itself a very strained and strenuous procedure) but it was in fact I and not Brighid who laboured with him to get out the sentence "I am slowly understanding reasons for my handicap." Brighid's notes state that he went completely limp after his gyrating exertions with me.

The second error in my recollection is that it wasn't until the following evening that he wrote the poem 'Magical Kinaesthesis' with Brighid. This poem would have involved all the battles, cajolery and wear and tear on Brighid which I described in the first chapter as she tried to tease out his lunging efforts to spell out complicated words. For instance, 'kinaesthesis' came out as 'kinasthdesus' which he explained as meaning "when balanz and movment coxhist". He claimed he heard it on the television. When asked what exactly he was saying in the poem, his reply was "God started the younivers."

Shortly after the Hawking evening, Brighid discontinued the notebooks, mainly because some of the themes that came up in chats between herself and Davoren were very private and not fitting to be pasted down in a book to be shown around publicly. In addition, bearing in mind that while every phrase out of Davoren cost dearly in terms of energy and time, his comments and poems had begun to grow into an avalanche.

The other principal change that took place was that Brighid and I became more dogged in backing Davoren. We realised that we had an intelligent son who needed appropriate education and fostering, in spite of the fact that specialists were divided over his abilities. But even more we were becoming slowly and fearfully convinced that Davoren's was a voice in our midst which was clamouring to break out of the confines of our little house in Drumcondra. Davoren's "little sound" "greatly mystifying to knowledgeable minds", already reverberating powerfully through our lives, was soon to resound with a passionate plea in a wider world.

Hope   Igniting   Hearts

Perhaps no expectation of happiness
alights on your shoulder like a wagtail;
hope quivering throughout my entire being
shall ignite your passionate hearts.

This was Davoren's New Year wish for us in 1984. Earlier he had wished Brighid "a happy and successful old age" on her birthday on 18th December, lauding her in her Christmas Birthday poem as "a lady whose patience never ebbed". On Christmas Day he had written "slowly it appears the long vigil is over." Brighid recorded: "it was the first Christmas that we knew how he felt about the event. He threw himself enthusiastically into the spirit of Christmas."

It was a time for taking stock. Like the Burren rock to which his name alludes, there was layer upon layer of disturbances and eruptions being laid one upon another as his hitherto untapped energies spouted forth. There was the scandal of his assessment and placement as mentally handicapped while all the time Davoren was bursting with both ideas and fury. There was the backlog of harrowing experiences which Davoren had locked away in his heart. There was the freakish discrepancy between our simple delight at Davoren being able to communicate at all and our bewilderment at this child who seemed to behave like an oracle in our midst.

But the inter-locking layers of Davoren's and our dilemmas were not laid out in serene stasis like the compacted Burren slabs. Rather it was a living drama in which the three of us were often pulling in different directions. Davoren was passionate and angry but strangely sly and devious in making his case, Brighid engaged in a forceful and sustained campaign to advocate Davoren's cause while I tended to be diplomatic, bordering on passive, although when I got a sense that Davoren's talents and future were really being thwarted, I could be explosively fierce.

Nevertheless, at the beginning of 1984, we were hopeful that, having found his voice, Davoren could somehow progress through normal channels. As Davoren moved into his tenth year, we still dreamed dreams of the crooked ways being made straight and the rough roads being made smooth.

The first normal channel that we wanted to open up for Davoren was for him to begin to have an education. Despite the precocity of some of his statements, we knew that there were immense lacunae in his knowledge and development. He ardently wished to move away from the mentally handicapped environment in which he had been placed up to now, even though he had many friends and great loving care at St Michael's House Day Development Centre in Ballymun.

Our first goal, and it was a limited one, was to have him transferred to the school in the Central Remedial Clinic. This was Davoren's 'much-voiced' dream too during that spring of 1984. Given the extent of Davoren's handicap and the extreme fragility of his communication lifeline, integrating him into a normal school was still only a gleam in the mind's eye at this stage, even for passionate dreamers like Brighid and Davoren. I must confess that I was often faint-hearted and pessimistic about our chances of getting Davoren fully accepted; the extremes of his immobility and powerlessness on the one hand and expressiveness and giftedness on the other were such that it would be like trying to get a camel through the eye of a needle.

The fetishism of testing was the main obstacle we faced. Brighid and I argued very strongly for a different approach. We felt that pouncing on Davoren *and* Brighid in a spirit of testing introduced a whole series of tensions into a working relationship which depended on finding a delicate balance of relaxation and stimulation. It was an intervention which set in train a resistance (whether willed or not in Davoren does not matter), that vitiated the very possibility of Davoren communicating at all. Instead we issued an open invitation for prolonged and intensive observation of Davoren working with Brighid and the other helpers in our own home. The deadlock was finally broken by just such a visit by one of the CRC psychologists after which Davoren was admitted to the CRC school. Our hopes for normal channels opening up for him had been dented but were not entirely dashed.

Our difficulty with psychologists was not only fateful for Davoren's prospects but also the most dramatic example of the way in which he was a 'sign of contradiction' for experts. Our experience was that receptivity to Davoren's personality and unique way of communicating was no respecter of training or background, but more a case of the spirit blowing where it willed. At the beginning it was very difficult to accept the randomness whereby one person who might have no special expertise about handicap was immediately at ease with his communicating while another person, eminently qualified or working in the field, was disconcerted and helpless with him. More generally, we found that people coming fresh to him would often adopt a 'no problem' attitude to his transport, feeding or communication needs, for example, while those working with handicapped people saw difficulties everywhere. That Davoren was uniquely difficult (which he was) was their attitude. Facilities which were tailored to the needs of 'normal' handicapped children could not be adapted to cope with Davoren.

Brighid, and to a lesser extent Davoren, remained combative and intransigent towards the nay-sayers and those placing obstacles in his path. I was aware that there were difficulties in that approach, in making acceptance or non-acceptance of Davoren a touchstone in our own dealings with others. Yet while I was very little concerned at this early stage that people recognise his special poetic gifts, I did get upset at their blindness to the fire in his eyes and to the spirited intelligent energy coursing through him.

Brighid had a tendency to become angry and explosive if friends, relatives, workers in the handicap services or neighbours didn't treat Davoren well. At times she operated on the principle of giving people one chance. This often meant that she would involve Davoren somehow in the conversation, say by sitting him on her lap and typing with him. But if this reaching out to the blind wasn't reciprocated by the target of her demonstration, she could be a bit brusque and unforgiving.

I had three good reasons for not adopting this 'take no prisoners' approach. One was that I had my bad moments with Davoren myself. If I lifted him, held him in my arms or interacted with him physically there was no distancing effect. I might be upset or emotional but I was inside the intimidating walls of his disability. But standing at a certain remove from Davoren, I too could be transfixed or paralysed by horror at his helplessness. There is an element in all of us that is not able to cope with powerlessness. We each have different strengths and blind spots which either empower us or cripple us in penetrating the apparent helplessness of extreme physical handicap.

The second reason for my reserve was that several people who were very close to me experienced excruciating distress in the presence of Davoren. My father, even after Davoren's public triumphs, never quite got beyond the 'God help us' stage with him and, to my recollection, never directly addressed him in his life. This was hurtful as he took a fairly keen interest in the doings of his other grandchildren.

Another good friend of mine, John Doyle, was also stricken with immobility when confronted by Davoren. This was quite painful for me as I met John quite often with Davoren. We used to go on long circling walks in the Botanic Gardens, discussing philosophy or John's teaching work with children, at both of which he was exceptionally gifted. These walks became another element in the Davoren legend, being blamed for the style and vocabulary of his religious questioning and for his preoccupation with the limitations of philosophy. Like all good legends, it had a strong element of truth. I would stop every so often on these walks, often enough in front of the statue of Socrates near the weir on the Tolka, and try to include Davoren in the dialogue. For the most part, John would look blankly at me. After a while I would realise that my efforts were fruitless and we would continue our walk and conversation, carrying on as if Davoren was scarcely there at all. And in truth, it often appeared that way due to the strongly relational aspect of Davoren's emergence as a personality *and* as someone who could communicate, albeit with horrendous difficulty. Davoren had powerful antennae but he could switch off or appear completely switched off when he wanted to. If he felt that someone was closing him out, he would pull down the shutters and effectively that meant there was nobody at home.

Davoren wrote a poem for John called 'Your Quintessential Traits', which brought about a reconciliation of sorts. John had explained that he was not by nature 'a believer'. Davoren wrote: "At one with snowdrops/ appeasing winter gods'/ lengthy domination and wrath/ you sought a pathway/ 'twixt faith and scepticism —/ treading warily with sandals/ of tremulous belief." John's response to the poem was, "Bull's-eye!"

The third reason for my disquiet was connected very intimately with this vulnerability of Davoren to the responses of others, especially children. One of the greatest shattering of illusions in my life was to witness how nakedly awe-struck and often horror-struck most children were on first meeting Davoren. He hungered and thirsted for contact with boys and girls of his own age while he persecuted us with requests for a brother or sister. You can imagine the bitter cup of disappointment for him when he went among a group of children and found them appalled by him. Younger children would approach him gingerly to have a good stare and then run back in fright to their mothers. I recall vividly bringing him to children's shows where he ended up being the main spectacle. What was happening on the stage would be forgotten as they turned to their parents or nudged their friends to draw their attention to the floor show going on behind them. Embarrassed parents would try to divert the children's attention back to the main entertainment but after a while the heads would turn again to the freak peep-show.

With older children, the blighted hope of engagement would play out differently. Too nonchalant to show such an obvious interest, they might even say 'hello' to him if introduced, but after a short while his lack of physical reaction and his inability to move to the heart of the action would render him uninteresting to them and they would go on their way, scavenging the world for challenge and experience. It was only the exceptional child who could cut through these extreme reactions of fright or indifference and come close, touch him and speak to him naturally. Generally it needed sensitive parents or adults to gently guide the children's perception. Gradually I came to accept that there was something primitive but unassailable about these reactions of children; it takes a rare breadth of the human spirit to see into the heart of personality behind severe handicap and disfigurement.

Davoren's reaching out to children was not confined to inner yearning. On occasions when he found himself among children with whom he desperately wanted to engage, he would often get quite agitated, shifting about so much that a little sound, an 'ah' or a gurgle, could be heard with the exhale of his breath. I could see clearly a glimmer of expectation in his eyes as if he thought that his little sound would reassure the frightened child or hail the indifferent one. With some, those with special acumen, his breathy 'voice' worked and they could feel him talking to them but for most, it confirmed their first impressions — for the affrighted ones he was a freak, for the bored ones he was just like a baby.

The effect on Davoren of these magical encounters on the one hand and dashed expectations on the other was cumulative. Where a friendship budded or blossomed, he could begin to sparkle, but when fear and neglect prevailed, he would withdraw dramatically into his own world, to his 'conversations in his head' or whatever.

□□□□

Davoren was rapturous at first with his entry into real school. This was his first experience of anything like a school day and while he had more than his share of difficulties with feeding and toileting and seizures during class, he coped quite well with the new schedule. While his ability to reach out to his classmates was severely limited (most of them would have a physical impairment but nothing like as chronic a communication difficulty), he received a warm welcome. But most important of all, he made an abiding friend. Mary Munnelly, bubbly, gregarious and chatty, was at ease with Davoren immediately. Two years younger than he, by coincidence her birthday was on the thirteenth of March while Davoren's was on the twelfth. For ever afterwards they celebrated their birthdays together. Mary chatted away to Davoren unselfconsciously. She loved to take charge of him, helping to feed him or taking him for a walk, for example (she could walk using something to support herself). But during the time she knew him, she passed from this mothering, slightly bossy role to a deeper appreciation and comradeship. She was not at all bookish but she thoroughly enjoyed the glow of his achievements.

The spirit of Davoren's first year at school in the CRC is well captured in a mainly light-hearted poem he wrote about a cookery class during his first year with teacher Joan Hayes, who was sensitive and eager to involve Davoren in every way possible. His new-found inclusion comes through but also his sense of isolation:

The Cookery Catastrophe

Sugar showered upon the floor,
eggs stuck to the ceiling;
trampled raisins all about
make sandwiches more appealing.
Watching castor sugar buns
rising in the oven
always gives me sad thoughts
and makes me full of longing.

But, by the time he entered his second year, the discrepancy between his self-expression at home with Brighid and the helpers and his relatively mute performance at school was becoming increasingly marked—in spite of their being enormous efforts made to assist him. Speech therapists and specialists in linking disabled people with computers through various types of switches deployed their full range of resources to guide him towards independent communication. There were even occasional flashes of hope such as the news bulletin which Joan Hayes sent home on 12th November 1984, announcing that Davoren had typed his name on the computer that day. But mechanical means of accessing Davoren's intelligence were unable to accommodate themselves to the variations in his muscle tone. Davoren seemed to need the electric charge of the human contact. As he put it colourfully himself many years later in an interview with a journalist, you can't compare the hard contours of a computer to a pair of "soft boobs". This was not a problem unique to Davoren as I learned later at a conference on technology-assisted communication for disabled people. One of the most provocative and interesting papers warned that too much faith in technology could be a blind alley for many disabled people with communication difficulties, unless a highly sensitive matching of communication systems to the unique preferences and sensitivities of the individual was central to all the experimentation.

Davoren's poem 'Paltry Victory' conveys very pithily the negative loop set in train by a stressful insistence that he make a "tremendous effort" to respond to the demands of technology:

> I keep asking a million muscles
> to dance just one little step
> at my command, but all in vain;
> perhaps tremendous effort
> amplifies and heightens my rather
> negligible attempts at moving.

In addition to these technical setbacks, there was a lingering suspicion about Davoren's communication that dated back to our difficulties in having him accepted as intelligent in the first place. For the most part this was expressed diplomatically: Let you continue to work with him at home in your way, while we get on with assessing his ability to develop independent communication. The sub-text was that independent communication was real communication. This bias showed itself in the low-key or non-committal way in which poems or homework were received in the classroom. Little triumphs which he was beginning to have outside of school were also down-played. We didn't mind that too much as we didn't want him to be over-fêted, but there was an absence of that sense of normal celebration accompanying the achievements of someone so handicapped.

Thus home and school worked on parallel tracks rather than in synchrony. This affected Brighid more than me as I had more frequent day-to-day contact with the school, going out once a week to assist with Davoren swimming, although that too had required a battle to set in place. It was a perfect pool, heated to a higher degree than a normal swimming pool, and when Davoren was supported by a ring, he could sometimes make some little movement, something like his 'little sound'. However, the main pleasure he and I got from it was to renew in the buoyancy of the water the ecstasy of our 'jumpy together'. Davoren used to get into a paroxysm of excitement as I built up the rhythm of our jumping in the splashy turbulence.

An amusing incident at the poolside one day illustrates some of the tensions of that time and our way of handling them. One particularly obstructive teacher made some cutting remark to me or Davoren. I can't remember what exactly it was, but it must have been strong as I tended to err on the side of diplomacy in my relations with CRC staff. Anyhow I felt obliged to make some riposte and a few stormy words were exchanged. I experienced an enormous compulsion to throw the teacher into the pool. It was one of the strongest impulses to violence I had ever felt and I had to resort to counting to ten or saying a quick prayer in order to deflect it. I got together with Davoren in the pool and whispered to him about my surge of fury and we laughed together. We threw ourselves with extra zest into our jumping and splashing.

"The hassle of the lack of communication in the classroom is getting me down" was one of Davoren's printable responses to his plight. In giving his side of the story, I would not want in any way to underplay his own responsibility for some elements in his predicament. Trenchant as Brighid could be at times with those who she felt were not giving Davoren a fair hearing, her battles with Davoren were equally unrelenting. Her earnest wish to the end of her days, both for Davoren and for herself, was that he find an independent means of communication. The last thing she wanted was to be chained to him for life. Tears of frustration on both sides, followed by the inevitable tears of reconciliation, followed in turn by playful repartee, were often the pattern of these exchanges.

A striking epiphany of optimism occurred at the beginning of his second year when he entered the class of Treasa McManus, who had a strong personal interest in literature and drama. Shortly after beginning in her class, he reported back one day: "Satisfaction never before acknowledged as teacher read my poems!" Implicitly this was a sign that poems written at home, which were often his version of homework, were not being read in class. He was hopeful of having "a spellbinding year". He was so moved that he wrote a poem called 'Enchantress' for Treasa that evening, in which he imagined "sunbursts of light" penetrating "the dark depths of the ocean" and "tender mermaids ... combing mysterious dreams from hair infinitely long".

Another major crisis at the CRC concerned his making of his First Holy Communion. Questions were raised by the priest involved about Davoren's understanding of what was involved. This querying of his right to receive his First Communion had no connection with the clergy in our own parish, who were always very welcoming towards Davoren. Brighid, who had extreme difficulty with the patriarchal church, nevertheless identified very strongly with the great themes and feasts of Christianity and was occasionally tempted back to find nourishment as, for example, at the Easter Vigil Mass. Almost invariably she was disappointed, so the only religious services we ever attended as a family were the sung Mass in the Pro-Cathedral on Sunday with the Palestrina Choir and, at an earlier period, a similar Mass with the St James's Choir in Westland Row. Getting out to these Sunday ceremonies depended very much on Davoren's morning rituals going smoothly, so it was a very occasional event.

I, on the other hand, had a much more umbilical attachment to the Church despite huge reservations, mainly shared with Brighid. The psalms and the sayings and parables of Jesus and to a lesser extent the letters of Paul were deeply inscribed in my heart; they summoned me to hearken to the best side of myself and it seemed an abomination to be cut off from whatever might sustain that core of myself. So I quite frequently brought Davoren to Mass and he insisted, in an interesting exchange with Brighid, that he wanted to go to our local parish church. He accused Brighid of being cynical about religion and of not understanding the need to go on pilgrimages, both of which charges she rejected. He said "Mass is simply a way of solemnising our relationship with God," and was not satisfied with what he perceived as Brighid's dilettantish trips to the Pro-Cathedral.

But I also liked to bring Davoren to the church on my own as it was a place to be quiet with him. I used to be able to ventilate in prayer or anti-prayer my difficulties with my beloved son (before God, if you like, but I wasn't very sure of that) and still at the same time feel very close to him. Davoren was mainly hushed and attentive in church; a look of awe came over his face. If he had particular discomfort in his chair, I would take him on my lap, put my arms around him and feel even closer to him. I would often weep sitting there with him and we seemed to achieve a deeper understanding of one another there than almost anywhere else, apart from on our outdoor adventures. It eased the pain of my difficulties at home with him in front of the typewriter.

The apogee of Davoren's confronting us about religion came when he had the gall to write a poem entitled, 'I Wish I Was a Catholic'. Davoren knew that displays of unflinching orthodoxy were certain to provoke a strong reaction, from Brighid particularly. He also played mercilessly on this raw nerve when he got together with his godmother, Anne D'Art, who debated forcefully with Brighid from a traditional Catholic perspective ("prevailing ideologies do not attract your questioning heart," he wrote of Anne). He responded very strongly to the vibrancy of Anne's voice, loved her dearly but also enjoyed embroiling her in his efforts to outrage his parents.

The religious culture in which we were steeped is well illustrated by the Latin tag we used to describe one of Davoren's most characteristic postures, especially when he was very young. "*Dominus vobiscum*," we would intone as his folded fists shot up involuntarily to his shoulders when he was excited. Even though technically the gesture was an uncontrolled muscular contraction, we saw it as an open, expansive invitation to share in his delight.

Brighid's combative attitude towards many aspects of the Church did not in any way lessen her resolve when she saw one of her son's dreams being hindered. In fact, all three of us saw the whole First Communion matter as an incredible example of a priest being fussy and legalistic, even apart from any special claims for Davoren's intelligence. Brighid was, however, particularly angry at the affront to Davoren and never was her advocacy more impassioned and bitter. Because of all his hospitalisations and his being cut off from schooling, Davoren was in fact older than most children in making his First Communion. The whole wrangle was sweetened in the end by Davoren writing one of his most moving poems — 'Half Loaves' — for the occasion. It was an especially happy day for

me as it was the last public occasion in Davoren's life that my mother was
well enough to attend.

The bells pealed loudly
as children pinioned
by chair and calipers
limped or wheeled into church.

Poignant scenes awaited
gathering onlookers
while photographers
froze the spectacle in time.

Timidly mothers smiled
trying to look inconspicuous
as public eyes gazed
in naked curiosity.

The priest obliged
with goblet of wine
but I wanted to taste
the loaf of suffering.

Pictures show my smile
but my hunger bit deep;
loneliness helmeted my heart
in case it broke.

Weep not, birds,
in song though I am mute,
my spirit sings with you
in praise of our maker.

The ironic aftermath of the ceremony was that it created a new strain
in my trips to Mass with him, when I used to have to bring him up to
receive Communion. I would have to make sure that the priest gave

Davoren only the tiniest fragment of the host, which would often remain visibly stuck on the tip on his tongue unless I worked it towards the back of his mouth. But I didn't feel able to receive Communion myself and so it accentuated in a public and painful way my love/estrangement relationship with the Church.

Later on his friends, Paul and Brian Coffey, and later on again, Barry McCormack, used to bring him to Saturday evening Mass. Going out with the lads, especially on dark, wintry nights, was an independent adventure in itself and on the return to the house, there would be the chat, jokes and repartee, with Paul in particular specialising in his deadpan style of telling jokes. Davoren used to try to join in by making up his own jokes, which were mostly terrible in all senses of the word.

□□□□

Throughout all these years of involvement with the CRC, with their fair share of turbulence, there was one abiding presence, whose support was wholehearted and solidly down-to-earth. After the initial doctor's diagnosis and referral in 1976, we were put in the hands of physiotherapist Kay Keating. Kay (whom while we were dealing with her officially, we never called anything but Miss Keating—she inspired such respect) was the rock in the CRC who never failed us. A strong Kerry woman, she was head of the physiotherapy department, so our first dealings with her were on the mats in the therapy room as she gently but firmly rotated Davoren's spine. Even though the scoliosis on his spine was one of his problems that undid him in the end, ever afterwards when she worked with Davoren on the floor, she complimented him and us on the way we had ensured that his spine remained supple in spite of the severity of his handicap. She mainly put it down to the immense amount of handling he received at home, the time he spent on the famous laps, working or being cuddled by us or by his many girl friends. Miss Keating's praise of Davoren's spine was one of those odd reassuring mantras which sustained us in bleak times.

But she became for us much more than a hands-on and shepherding physiotherapist. Particularly for Brighid, she became a counsellor and fortifier. I had intense admiration for her and enjoyed her candid ways, but with her strong approach to discipline with her staff she didn't fit into my mould of 'the ideal counsellor'; for Brighid, however, she was perfect. Even though communication problems were not her professional forte, she encouraged us endlessly, yet always matched that encouragement with sound practical advice. Davoren was, I always felt, slightly intimidated by her. She must have been an awe-inspiring presence when he first encountered her as a helpless babe on those exercise mats in the CRC gymnasium.

The insistent theme which unfolded during those years of Davoren's life was that his handicap was so un-normal that normal channels for enabling him to overcome his disability would not work for him. The paradoxical outcome to that insight was that Davoren and Brighid set their hearts on finding a place for him within normal schooling. Integration became the new and inspiring melody in his life which he and Brighid, and eventually and reluctantly I, pushed to the limit for the rest of his life.

Shimmying Towards the Light

At eleven o'clock on the night before Christmas Eve in 1984, we found ourselves a few miles outside Maam Cross in the driving rain on our way to join friends Barbara Callan and Dave Hogan and their toddler son Kevin in Letterfrack. My battered Renault 4, the third in the line, was taking a pounding in the sheets of rain sweeping in upon us. Suddenly there was an awful rending noise from one side of the car. I stopped and got out while Brighid and Davoren shivered inside, as several holes in the floor made it impossible to properly heat the car.

Nothing had fallen off and we didn't have a flat tyre. There was no passing traffic that I could call on for help so I decided we would have to try to proceed. We limped along the remaining twenty-five miles with this horrendous noise grinding in our ears (it turned out that one of the front wheel bearings had gone). The household had retired to bed when we arrived well after midnight but magic was restored and our shattered nerves soothed as Barbara made tea for us while Dave lit candles on branches of the thirteen sacred trees of Ireland (the birch, rowan, ash, alder, willow, hawthorn, oak, holly, hazel, vine, ivy, dwarf elder and elder, corresponding to the thirteen consonants of the Celtic alphabet), which they had suspended from the ceiling.

I had taken redundancy from Telecom Eireann and was trying to find my feet as a free-lance journalist but I felt a good break over Christmas was well warranted. In fact this was my first Christmas free of work for a long time as duties at the International Telephone Exchange usually involved being rostered over the holiday, and I had been very conscious of the hardship that this rota had imposed on Brighid and Davoren. Brighid had a great love of Christmas but was finding it increasingly stressful over the years. Davoren had twice spent Christmas Day in hospital and the season had an indelible link with her mother's death

69

which occurred at the end of December a few months after I first met Brighid.

Davoren was just over nine-and-a-half years old but in my recollection, that Christmas in Letterfrack he was at the height of his powers. His own poem on his life, 'My Life, My Voice, My Story,' talked of lines pouring through his veins. Over those few blessed days, poems, mischief, love and celebration shot out from Davoren's eyes and limbs, if we can speak thus of someone so crippled. Brighid's file for the holiday contains eleven poems written over a period of five or six days. It does not matter if they do not stand up to scrutiny as poems in the cold light of post-festive winter but as expressions — proofs if you like — of his inner spiritual vitality, they remained with me as an important testimony for the rest of his days, and remain with me still.

He started with a settling-in poem on Christmas Eve, entitled 'Letterfrack Lovers' Leap,' which concluded with the lines: "Amazing light breaking over russet crags/ lifts our weary city-poisoned hearts/ and turns our limbs into Leda's wings." This was rich, given our car problems; taking flight might be our only way of getting home. Crisp, frosty weather had set in by Christmas Day, perfect for walking if you were well wrapped-up. At nightfall a startlingly bright full moon shone over the hills. But it was the atmosphere in the house on Christmas Day that really sparked Davoren into life. Kevin's clambering was a great joy to Barbara and Dave, and I think Davoren felt very much part of it since Barbara had chatted so much about Kevin on her Dublin visits. Dave was the chef and liked to warm to his task with some excellent home-made wine. There were also many other bottles of port, spirits and liqueurs received as presents. There was a great deal of toasting — Kevin's walking, Davoren's communication, my new career as a journalist, Brighid's studies, Dubliners Barbara and Dave settling in the West, and so forth. Davoren was in the mood for guzzling and, despite the fact that he could only take sips, had a taste of anything that was going. On that particular day, his digestive system and ability to drink were in fine fettle, so by the time the meal was coming to an end, I am convinced he had absorbed quite an amount of alcohol in proportion to his small frame. The music was also flowing freely by this stage as both Barbara and David played several instruments and sang. This roused Davoren to compose a drinking ballad which was prefaced by a "Piss off!" exclamation when Brighid protested, "Not another poem" (by then he was on his fourth).

Lines Written in Elation

Plastered I was when first I came
to sing my party piece. Nnaa...
Plonk-drunk I lay in a haze
of alcoholic laughter. Nnaa...

Pissed I was until I heard
the crowing of the cock. Nnaa...
Longing for some liquor,
to the tavern I went back. Nnaa...

This was sung with great gusto to some general ballad air that I cannot recall. There was no stopping Davoren now. For someone who was so often limp and exhausted from coughing and strained breathing, he could have amazing stamina when he was buoyed up by loving friends. His capacity to forge on regardless on these occasions put a great strain on Brighid's energies. There were no more poems that day, just joking and cajoling. Brighid gave him her full measure; for her, too, this was a Christmas that would wipe away painful memories. I stood by in the wings, ready to take over when she collapsed.

The next day there was a light covering of snow on the hills and, as a precautionary measure, Dave decided he had better check out the deer, which had recently been transferred to the Connemara National Park, where he worked at that time. We decided we would take turns to carry Davoren and Kevin up the Diamond, the peak which dominates the village, to locate the deer. This of course had to be celebrated in another poem, written in a mock-heroic style and full of exaggeration and hyperbole. Nevertheless it ends beautifully with these lines:

Azure skies beflecked
with skeins of snow
amaze our loam-coloured eyes
and close by, our deer shyly wait.

We met many of Barbara and David's friends and their children. Davoren gloried in being the centre of attraction, alongside Kevin of course. Truth to tell, we were so happy for him that we didn't put many restraints on him. He charmed the ladies as usual, one of whom, Eithne, received one of his characteristically searing and adulatory poem-addresses. It ends: "Pine needles have pierced/ your tender soul/ as life's path/ proves painfully thorny."

The other main adventure of the holiday, apart from treks in and out to Clifden to get the car patched up, was horse-riding for Davoren with friends on a farm overlooking Cleggan Bay. Dave held Davoren on the huge but docile mare and, although he was not entirely comfortable because of the strain on his hips straddling the horse, he enjoyed the experience mightily. This gave rise to poem number seven in which innocent boyishness and inflated comparisons jostle with one another.

> All night long I dreamed
> of livid nostrils flaring
> and lively hooves clip-clopping;
> Petrarch could not have written
> sonnets on how life-enhancing
> or Promethean was my moment
> of glorious liberation on horseback.

Davoren's farewell poem to Connemara contained the lines: "As I leave you all, sad sap pours from my bole." This echoed all our feelings but we were mainly rejuvenated for the fray. For me in particular, the days away from the routines of telephone work and from the new stresses of freelancing gave me a fresh insight into Davoren's aspirations. I realised afresh how crushing his existence had been inhaling "the noxious fumes of platitudes, misunderstanding and misdiagnosis" during his early years. As it is for us all, the need to express himself was as vital for Davoren as breathing, but unfortunately meeting that need was as strained and hazardous as his chaotic gasping and puffing. I could see plainly that Davoren and Brighid had initiated a great enterprise and that I would have to row in with them, no matter what the resistance and begrudgery.

◻◻◻◻

Away from school with its battles for acceptance and affirmation, two other channels opened up in Davoren's life around this time — one public and celebratory and the other secret and mysterious. While Brighid and Davoren became co-conspirators in a mission to spread his voice outside the confines of the home, in the intimate circle of the home Davoren became more oracular as he began to tell us of his conversations with various historical personages.

Going public with Davoren's poetry was an admission by us that his degree of handicap and complexity of mind were such that he would never make progress through normal channels. Brighid and I had realised that something was taking place—around our Bantry Road hearth with all its homely chaos and gnawing anxiety—that was bigger than either of us. Davoren's defiant and distinctive 'voice' demanded a hearing, yet it was trapped in a kind of limbo because it didn't satisfy the experts' criteria of independence. We were calling out for help but we felt we were being met by, at best, 'at arm's length' toleration or at worst, jaundiced indifference. Within the world of handicap services, Davoren and Brighid were viewed as an exotic conundrum or as eccentric nuisances. Thus it was that Brighid began to ferret out channels for Davoren which would bring his name and dilemma to a wider public.

Davoren entered several poems for the Irish Schools Creative Writing Awards in 1985. In theory this competition was outside Davoren's range, since he was just turning ten and was still floundering in the CRC Primary School while this scheme, organised by the Community and Comprehensive Schools Sports and Cultural Association, was intended for older children. Nevertheless two of his poems were selected by the judges for praise, 'Utter Tranquillity' winning first prize in the junior poetry section while 'Winter Landscapes' was highly commended.

'Utter Tranquillity' dealt with Davoren's wheelchair confinement and his religious questioning in startling images for a ten-year-old child. Its background is best explained in Brighid's notes:

Davoren was watching a programme on ancient monastic sites in Ireland. Shortly afterwards he announced, "I would hope someday to be a monk." When asked why, he said: "I think prayer must renew Western man's faith." I said that this was very abstract. "Where did he get the idea of being a monk? What did he feel about being a monk?"

The poem is a reply to this question:

> *Tragic lives are*
> *transformed in contemplation*
> *of God's inscrutability;*
> *thereby equilibrium is restored.*
>
> *When a physically handicapped*
> *soul enters the kingdom*
> *of heaven, I wonder*
> *is God in a wheelchair?*
>
> *I want a life of*
> *passionate suffering*
> *and of joyfulness;*
> *don't deny me pain.*
>
> *Aquinas sleeps*
> *and leaves fall on*
> *his lonely grave;*
> *let me take monastic vows.*

Part of the prize for the winners was a day-long writing workshop. Davoren relished being in the thick of the action as he fell and lunged towards his keyboard during the writing exercises with Brighid and his other writing helper of the time, Audrey O'Loughlin. For once he enjoyed being the centre of attention as his fellow award-winners looked on in amazement at his thrashing wild-eyed movement and gave his every word special consideration. Belying the adult caricature of writers as competitive and egotistical, the other participants were a co-operative and lively bunch who adapted more sensitively than most of their peers to Davoren's unusual presence. Sara Berkeley, the highly talented winner of the senior poetry section, was warmly and gently encouraging and Davoren made special friends with Trevor Clohessy, an Irish-language winner from Connemara. They corresponded for several years afterwards. Ironically, in the light of his passion to be a monk, he basked in his usual fashion in the interest, care and appreciation of the girls. As his special guest, he brought along his CRC school friend Mary Munnelly, who took a shy delight in appearing in the press photographs with Davoren and his trophy. Davoren's poem to honour the occasion combined a sense of solemn awe with an honest admission of wolfish desire. It concluded: "Taste of glory/ sweet in my wordless mouth/ I savour hungrily, knowing I shall want more./ Listen song-birds, you are not/ the only choristers/ who can purple the heavens/ with your ecstasy."

John F Deane, founder of Poetry Ireland and chief judge in the poetry section, took a great interest in Davoren's themes and, while extremely discreet and unpushy, was very keen to see him develop his talents. No less than anyone else, he could not escape being chilled to the core at the extent of Davoren's handicap and the fragility of his hold on communication. He also knew that you could never draw a neat line between Davoren the aspiring writer and Davoren the profoundly handicapped boy. Nevertheless, it seemed to us that it was primarily to Davoren's strange vision as a writer that he was drawn. Over the next few years, Davoren got into the habit of going to poetry readings organised by Poetry Ireland and he was always given a warm and unfussy welcome. His occasional gurgling noises and hasty departures if he had an uncontrollable convulsion during a reverent poetry reading were accepted very matter of factly. The line of directors of Poetry Ireland, from John F Deane, to Rory Brennan and Theo Dorgan, made him feel very much part of a community.

Earlier in 1985 Davoren had had his first poem published when the *Irish Times* accepted a Christmas poem, 'Winter Landscapes', the same poem commended by the Irish Schools Creative Writing Awards judges. This gave him a great boost, especially after he thought it wasn't going to be published when Christmas went by without the poem appearing. The last two lines of the poem, with their striking echo of Yeats's 'Second

Coming,' have a note of pessimism not found in his more buoyant, childlike expressions of religious faith. "Womb-weary, Christ emerges anaesthetised/ searching in vain for Bethlehem's familiar hearth." The winning entries in the schools' writing competition were published in book form later in the year and he suddenly had a taste for the buzz of publication and success.

Brighid and I were delighted that Davoren first came to public notice as a young writer being encouraged to persevere with his writing alongside his peers, but we were not so naïve as not to realise that the light of publicity which he attracted was almost entirely due to his writing having emerged out of such a profound handicap. On the other hand, if it were not for Davoren's handicap, neither Brighid nor I would have hustled so hard for him. I can honestly say that it was in neither of our natures to push a young person prematurely into the limelight. As a teacher, Brighid's attitude was that young talent should be fostered and celebrated but that it was nevertheless a fragile growth. In normal circumstances, I would probably be excessively hesitant about courting publicity for a young child. If any normal channels could have been foreseen for Davoren, we would have been content to take a back seat and let him be directed by other guides, such as teachers or more experienced writers. The brutal truth of the matter was that we had to do the advocacy for Davoren, and that doing so was becoming an urgent imperative in view of the questioning and scrutiny of his intelligence and of the in-built limitations of his method of writing as he grew bigger and more awkward.

These conflicts were sharpened considerably by the next enlargement of Davoren's public profile when he won a major award in the British Spastic Society's National Literary Awards in 1986. This occasion involved a flight to London, the first of Davoren's many trips abroad, but more dramatically it turned the spotlight of British television on our home and Davoren's life. Zoe Brown, a BBC Breakfast Time presenter, who was one of the judges, described his poems as "amazing in their maturity and literary quality". ITN came and filmed Davoren working at his typewriter at home and on jaunts around the city with me. Despite my recent entry into journalism, this was my first participative experience of how the media stages certain events, which both reveal and conceal the truth of the matter. I was filmed reading to Davoren on Paddy Kavanagh's seat on the Grand Canal (the old one, that is, by the lock at Baggot Street), a scene which was plausible because the canal bank walk had a huge symbolic significance for Brighid and me as it was there that I had proposed to her. It was on those "leafy-with-love" banks that I had first been enraptured "in a web of fabulous grass and eternal voices by a beech", had accepted the need to "feed the gaping need of my senses", and been given "ad lib to pray unselfconsciously with overflowing speech".

Davoren's own reaction on hearing the news of his London win celebrated the break in the bleakness which still surrounded so much of his life in a little hymn of religious praise.

> *Exultate, jubilate.*
> *Show thy heartbeat, sun,*
> *warm the frozen-fingered reeds—*
> *shivering mourners at winter's demise.*
> *Yesterday winds blew chill and*
> *raw self-doubt seared my soul;*
> *but exultant today*
> *the Sovereign Son I sing.*

❑❑❑❑

Prior to going to London, I had another major crisis in my espousal of Davoren's cause. Suddenly the scale of publicity for, and attention on, Davoren seemed to be getting out of hand—and I was worried that we would be vulnerable without additional official backing from the organisations dealing with handicapped children in Ireland. In addition, I had long been toying with the idea of writing something about Davoren's communication predicament. After graduating with my diploma in journalism in 1983, I had spent a year as a freelance journalist, chasing stories and shifts in various newspapers. It had been a difficult but exhilarating time, trying to juggle the demands of making a living and being available for Davoren's emergencies. In a sense I was operating with a ball-and-chain around my ankles: for to really make a go of being a freelance, you need to be available to work odd hours and go anywhere. Moreover I had come to realise that while I racked my brains to find arresting material, all the time the real drama was unfolding around my own hearth.

In December 1985, I obtained a full-time appointment with the *Irish Press* as a sub-editor, which relieved me of the strain of hustling for a living. The only disadvantage was that it involved evening and night work which re-introduced the strain of nights without back-up on Brighid. Yet once I settled into the new job, I thought I would go back to the project of exploring and writing about Davoren.

At this time Brighid and I also followed up leads hither and thither on alternative communication systems for people with disabilities. We also explored research findings on strange phenomena associated with people in whom the corpus callosum had been cut. One researcher proposes that "it is entirely possible that if a human brain were divided in a very young person, both hemispheres could as a result separately and independently develop mental functions of a high order at the level attained only in the left hemisphere of normal individuals." While we thought we might be able to shed light on Davoren's bizarre cast of mind, pressure of events turned us away from these researches.

With the growing swell of media interest in Davoren, I decided it would be timely to try a preliminary stab at fathoming Davoren myself. Thus I began to pore over all the scraps of paper on which his poems and conversations were scattered, the orderly and comprehensive notebooks of the early days having given way under the 'torrent' of communication to a much more chaotic array of material. Now communication could happen whenever and wherever a helper was available. In addition the typewriter was often replaced by a letter-board with the alphabet in the standard 'qwerty' keyboard arrangement. This enabled the helper to distinguish more clearly the letter to which Davoren was pointing and was very convenient although it meant that sometimes poems and important conversations ended up being scribbled on old Christmas cards and on the backs of bills.

The work he did with Audrey O'Loughlin, the AnCo trainee who had accompanied him to the writing workshop in Dublin, was especially interesting because they had developed a more free-flowing (relatively speaking: considering Davoren's laborious procedures) style of typing than he had ever achieved with any of the other helpers up to that time. With Audrey I could see him unburdening himself in ways which were not possible within the constraining sight of his mother and father. Some of these conversations were private explorations of worries big and small, from concern about his appearance to fears about illness and death. Many of these intimate chats I am only uncovering now. They make a disconcerting potpourri of tenderness, anxiety and 'scallywaggery' (this had become one of his favourite words for his mischievous side). Flowery flattery of Audrey would give way to complaints about him being constipated and needing to do a 'shitty'. Such a descent from soaring passion to basic bodily functions was especially keenly felt as in order to facilitate Davoren's toileting, we (or the helper) had to hold him in a squatting position for a considerable period of time, often accompanied by squeals of pain.

Audrey's communication with Davoren was especially revealing to me as he wrote several poems with her. Yet there was no escaping the embarrassing fact that Brighid was his primary muse in the very strong sense that it was in a very intimate relationship with her that he found his poetic voice. Nor was there any disguising the uncanny way in which indirectly I too was a muse for him. I am still profoundly disconcerted but no longer surprised as I delve into the archives to discover how often he looked up to me as a poetic inspiration. It was precisely for these reasons that our principal aim was to break Davoren free from these incestuous clutches, to enable him to express himself independently so that he could be acknowledged for himself.

The poems that Davoren wrote with Audrey may not have been among his very best but they were 'spoken' in his own distinctive voice. Davoren could, when he was of a mind to, write for a particular audience; his personal addresses often fell into this category, combining some very clear and strong statement, usually of affirmation, and then often ending with a twist in his own idiom. A little poem for Audrey was in this style:

Audrey, you fill my poignant existence with love;
you give me hope to go on,
penetrating my sad, silent fugue
with your musical laughter.

Audrey was indeed a warm-hearted, inspiring girl whose foxy hair gave off a tantalising radiance as she sat in front of the keyboard guiding and restraining him. She had a discriminating intelligent approach to life but was not sophisticated in her tastes. Davoren captured something of her character in another little piece he wrote about anxious thoughts pirouetting madly inside his head. It concluded: "Answers never arise out of the pompous minds/ of the aristocratic doctors and professors./ Give me one intelligent, ordinary Audrey/ and I enlighten the universe!"

The poem written with Audrey which especially dispelled the grey pall of doubt and uncertainty in me was written about a fireworks display. Simple as it was, it had an explosive impact on my inertia.

Fireworks Whizzardry

Squibs burn brittle-bright in the newmooned night.
Catherine-wheels spin zany circles in the drunken sky.
Rockets ricochet with rumba-like rhythm
against the backdrop of velvety black
sequined with glittering lonely stars.
The spheres clap.

Thus fortified, I wrote an article for the *Irish Press*. The phrase in it which rings down the years at me concerns our battle to develop independent communication for him. I concluded: "I often wished he was just five per cent less handicapped." I later used a similar expression in a short piece I wrote when his book was published four years later: "At times like these I say to myself that I would be happy to accept a trade-off: let him be five per cent less handicapped and I would sacrifice half the poems (there are literally hundreds). But I know, and Davoren knows, that there are no such pacts in life." This fruitless pointless prayer nagged away at me, but basically I was ready in my heart to celebrate Davoren's achievements at home and abroad.

□□□□

We brought Cian Cafferky with us on the trip to London as a friend and ally for Davoren. Cian, a cross between Jack Kerouac, Francis of Assisi and the Pied Piper of Hamelin, was a young man who had become an inspirational figure to Davoren. Cian had spent his early adult years as a bit of a vagabond, soaking up experience and reading. When Davoren met him, he was working as a care-worker with the Marino Clinic in Bray. A holiday group, called the Happy Wanderers, had been set up by Maria Garvey, a spirited teacher in the clinic at the time, and it was on one of their excursions to Kerry that Davoren had met Cian. He and his girlfriend, Annette Healy, had become part of our lives; like many others, I'm sure they often wondered what they had become part of. Still Cian, despite his giftedness with children, and with Davoren in particular, had a nice line in caustic commentary which kept him sane in the midst of the hubbub surrounding Davoren in London. He knew the literary haunts, pubs and offbeat spots of London and he was going to be our guide for whatever free time we had.

We were put up by the Spastic Society in their hostel in Fitzroy Square, very conveniently located in the Bloomsbury district. The fuss and the hospitality which surrounded us were overwhelming. Even though there were several other worthy prize-winners who deserved to be fêted just as much, something about Davoren's impish charm and perhaps our Irishness made a huge impact. Monica Hart, who was PRO for the Spastic Society, attended sensitively to our every need, making sure we had the right to say 'no' to requests for interviews if we were worn out. Zoe Brown, a gorgeous redhead, was completely enraptured by Davoren and vied with Alison, another Spastic Society staff member, for the privilege of holding Davoren on her lap in the intervals between his typing with Brighid.

On the day of the award ceremony, we saw the 'Breakfast Time' and ITN lunchtime footage prior to leaving the hostel, so we were inured to the barrage of publicity as the day progressed. However, back at the hostel in the evening, a further shock was to come. With the dramatic fanfare of the ITN 'News at Ten' Davoren's story was flagged as the main item in the second half of the news. It was mesmerising to see our little domestic battles being beamed to millions.

We heard afterwards that Davoren's 'handicap hero' fable was flashed across the networks in the United States and that a radio interview with Brighid and myself was broadcast in Sydney, Australia. While Monica Hart did her best to screen the post coming to us, this exposure caused us problems later as we received batches of correspondence for months afterwards, some of it offering helpful suggestions, other letters proposing well-worn paths, and most just responding to Davoren's winsome personality as portrayed via the TV images.

We stayed on in London for several days to follow up various leads on Davoren's communication (including a preliminary assessment at the famous Great Ormond Street Hospital) and to see the sights. We brought Davoren to a classical concert in one of the great London concert halls, reliving for Brighid a time in her life when she worked in London as a penniless student and stood for the Proms in the Royal Albert Hall. Cian brought Davoren on expeditions to unusual bookshops and taverns. Despite these tourist adventures, however, my abiding memory of our first London trip was a quiet intimate moment back in the hostel one evening.

Brighid, who was spun out after the day's exertions, couldn't take any more of Davoren's high-flying exuberance. When he had been washed, toileted and made ready for bed, I brought him downstairs to give Brighid a rest, knowing that the night would bring restlessness as Davoren's strained breathing disturbed us and him. Despite his generally good health during those months, most nights still meant a vigil of draining his chest and clearing out his phlegm. The Spastic Society had installed an Apple computer in a room downstairs so I sat with Davoren in front of the keyboard. There were no gimmicks or switches. I just felt happy for Davoren and at ease with him. All my apprehensions about the London trip seemed to have been ill-founded although I knew that alarming expectations had been raised.

Suddenly it was easy to write with Davoren. His movements towards the letters were large and dramatic. He was animated and excited on my lap, compared to our usual tense and jerky exchanges in front of the keyboard. I cannot find the record of this chat with Davoren but I do remember that it was strong challenging stuff about the love and tensions between Brighid and myself, about the quest for peace within our restless and troubled hearts. I know that Davoren's curiosity and playfulness about sex came into it with his usual prophetic claims to see more clearly than we could ourselves.

Of course all this was expressed in a few pithy sentences because even with our unexpected fluidity that was all we could manage. But Davoren, even when he was not writing poetry, could still pack a powerful punch in a few phrases. That evening there was no resistance in me to what I often perceived as his posturing precocity. I didn't care if he was embarrassing me with fawning adulation or lacerating me with scathing darts. All that mattered was that I could feel the flow of urgent communication in a way which I hadn't experienced for a very long time.

As the years went by, my experiences of good communication with Davoren became more and more like that fleeting London epiphany — something I couldn't predict or control, something I had to wait on, like a blessing. I had to endure many dark and silent days and nights when all I had to fall back on were the memories of those graced moments when he was totally relaxed and I was totally relaxed and "hot tearfulness" was healed by the melody of his "little sound".

ꤷꤷꤷꤷ

Earlier in that May of 1986, Davoren had received a second prize in the Irish Schools Creative Writing Awards. This gave him a chance to renew some old acquaintances and to enjoy being just one among a group of very disparate young people interested in writing. John F Deane continued to offer gentle encouragement.

The following May Davoren won an award at the Cuirt 87 International Poetry Festival in Galway. At the presentation ceremony we met poet and entertainer Pat Ingoldsby, who was later to play an important, if quietly unobtrusive, role in helping to keep Davoren going. We stayed near the Spanish Arch and enjoyed the hundreds of swans on the river, the friendly atmosphere in the pubs and restaurants and wandering around the city to the official events and other informal gatherings. Travelling with Davoren, just as staying at home with him, could still be a very fraught affair, the strain of late-night events and hyper-activity with Davoren being compounded by distressed breathing and shrieking during the night, but for a year or two we were on a roll and the resurgence in Davoren's spirit made it all worthwhile.

An evening outing to a reading by the 1982 Pulitzer Prize-winning poet, the aptly-named Galway Kinnell, illustrates these difficulties. With the heat in the room, Davoren became distressed, moaning and crying as he gasped for air. Brighid and I brought him outside the room and comforted him. After a while I urged Brighid to go back in so that one of us at least could benefit from the occasion. Meanwhile I sat with Davoren outside in the foyer holding him on my knee with my arms wrapped around his chest, which often seemed to ease the strain on his breathing. I chatted to him and read from one of the books we had picked up during the day.

In a little consoling poem for me, Davoren had described this posture as "playfully letting us get/ to feel each other's hearts" and had urged me: "Put your strong arms round/ my little broken body/ and lilt your manly song." And holding him in that position outside the hotel room in which Galway Kinnell was reading had a special irony because one of the poems I most often intoned in his ear as I held him thus was a Kinnell poem, 'Saint Francis and the Sow', from that wonderful anthology, *The Rattle Bag*. It was like a prayer between us, telling of his loveliness despite and even in the midst of his drooling, choking, slobbering, grunting, pained shrieking and shitting. The poem is about everything flowering from within, of self-blessing; Kinnell imagines St Francis putting his hand on the creased forehead of the sow, and the sow "remembering all down her thick length, from the earthen snout...through the fodder and slops to the spiritual curl of the tail...the long, perfect loveliness of sow." As I read and celebrated his perfection, Davoren would lay his hand metaphorically on my brow and he would in turn bless me, in spite of my at times crabby and disappointed heart.

❑❑❑❑

At the end of that same May in 1986, he won an award for young writers at Listowel and so the Davoren Hanna caravan set off for North Kerry. Already late for the presentation ceremony, we very nearly didn't make it at all as we had a blow-out a few miles from Listowel. The following year Davoren went as a participant to Listowel, where on both occasions he took a very active part in the workshops. This was a great experience for him as on the one hand there was an atmosphere of attentive listening as his slowly typed contributions were awaited and read out, but also there were chastening suggestions for revision and re-working his poems in the workshop discussions. In general, I have to say that Davoren didn't take kindly to suggestions about revising his work; he would get fired up for a duel with this impertinent 'improver'. This was partly an act but a highly amusing one for us to witness as this cheeky pre-teenager faced down his advisors. In quieter less public moments, I think Davoren did take some advice and benefit from encouragement from poets Thomas McCarthy and Michael O'Loughlin.

Even though Davoren cast me in an exalted role as his inspiration, I never played an active role as a mentor to him with regard to his poetry. A slight puritanical streak in me sometimes made me think he was promiscuous with his poetic gifts and even with his emotions, as he gushed out his praises 'in poetic form' for some new person or experience, but mostly my chiding of him was gentle and only half-serious. Both Brighid and I often wished, however, that he would put a cap on his poetic output, as we felt we were already dealing with a poetry mountain, a surplus which the European Union was unlikely to take off our hands.

Still Davoren's opportunities for writing were so limited that he never seemed to want to go back over old ground. Occasionally, Brighid and he would have a discussion about a particular poem, with her suggesting, sometimes quite forcibly, that it wasn't working. Sometimes this would result in him following up her suggestions but more often than not he would either abandon the poem or go ahead and write what he wanted to write regardless.

The spirit of these and many other battles with Brighid is well captured in an early poem he wrote, taking her to task for talking about him (which we had to do all the time, even while deeply aware of its squirm-inducing effect on him) in a way which offended him. Brighid found the rebuke in the phrase 'flotsam thoughts' a bit hard to take, as he often accused her of being eclectic and of talking too much.

Mama, I love to experience me

When you edit my words
I am partly eclipsed,
even as I am affirmed.
Radical questions require
flotsam thoughts to metamorphose
into solid and sustaining answers.

The other highlight of our Listowel trips was meeting John B Keane. It was probably on our second trip that the conversation I remember most vividly took place. John B settled us into our seats, ordering a tiny glass of Guinness with a dash of blackcurrant for Davoren. Brighid started to tell John B about Davoren's growing preoccupation about sex; she explained that, although she worked in this area with teachers and mentally handicapped young adults, she felt someone like John B might be able to fill him in from a man's point of view. The conversation drifted off the subject but then John B leant down towards Davoren and whispered conspiratorially: "Have a good look around this pub" (which had quite a large proportion of mature ladies sitting around). "It's full of ladies' bottoms."

Later John B and Dav started a 'poem-throwing' contest. Unfortunately I do not have Davoren's contribution but John B's dashed-off contribution had great charm:

Welcome, dear Davoren,
young man without grouse.
You sweetened my feelings
and brightened my house.

On 29th September 1987, Davoren received the Christy Brown Award sponsored by Dublin Corporation. It was a privilege for Davoren to receive his award from the Lord Mayor, Carmencita Hederman, in the company of other bursary winners such as saxophonist Kenneth Edge. I cannot remember when we had introduced Davoren to Christy Brown's story, but by this stage he would have been very familiar with his 'Left Foot' predecessor. Receiving the award put a public spotlight on this line of disabled writers from Dublin, including his contemporary, Christopher Nolan. With some reservations Davoren was proud to carry on this tradition; one side of him wanted to be acknowledged as a writer pure and simple, while another side wanted to focus on the communication trap of ordinary disabled 'voices'. Davoren was mostly cocky enough to think that his writing was distinctive enough to hold its own in any company. I suspect he was a little bit more threatened by Christopher Nolan; on the one hand he feared that no one might want to publish his poems, Christopher having pre-empted the field; on the other hand he was worried that the extra notch on his own communication difficulties, compared to Christopher's, would eventually silence his voice. As chance would have it, we met Christopher and his father that very evening.

The day of the Christy Brown Award happened to be also the day for the conferring of the Freedom of the City on Dublin's cycling World Champion, Tour de France and Giro d'Italia winner, Stephen Roche. Like the rest of the country, Davoren, Brighid and I had followed Stephen's exploits over the summer, particularly the Tour de France win, and Davoren had fêted that event in his poem, 'Freewheeling Champ'. In chat at the Mansion House with Carmencita Hederman and the City Manager, Frank Feely, Dav's fascination with Stephen Roche's exploits came up and we received an invitation to the reception following the Freedom of the City ceremony. The carnival mood continued all day as we joined the crowds outside the Bank of Ireland for the colourful ceremony, eventually getting through the crushing throng into the wheelchair area, where we met Christopher Nolan. Later, inside the bank chambers, Davoren met Stephen and his wife, Lydia, an encounter which prompted another poem which concluded with the lines:

> *The two greeted each other*
> *from opposite sides of life's divide—*

the one from silver-spoked swift flight,
the other from the earthedness of words.

During these early years of public exposure, another drama was unfolding back at home, as the uncanny, mysterious side of Davoren's personality emerged more and more. One of Davoren's most well-loved poems, 'How the Earth Was Formed Quiz', introduced the character of Pliny the Elder, the Roman naturalist, who died in the midst of the destruction of Pompeii as Mount Vesuvius erupted. Pliny's enquiring mind was in full flight despite the danger as flames and lumps of molten lava flew through the air. The poem, which was written as homework for a geography class in school, marked the first poetic appearance of Pliny in our lives, but he had long been a teasing alter ego for Davoren who disclosed that he often had extensive conversations with Pliny going on in his head. Pliny was also a favourite refuge for him when he was pressed about where he came up with some of his most outlandish or oracular (depending on your point of view) pronouncements. "Pliny told me" or "I had a conversation with Pliny about it" became as common an explanation for the appearance in his writings of strange ideas as, in an earlier period, BBC Radio Three had been cited as the source of an unusual word.

At first we treated the visitations of Pliny as a bit of a joke and I in particular used to needle him about this rather fusty old character whom he had chosen as his interior conversational buddy. Davoren would sometimes give us licence to adopt this playful attitude by introducing his name in illogical contexts. For example one evening, when he was quite sick ("head hopping, ears ringing, chest pretty putrid, throat like a ploughed-up field"), he requested that he be brought back to bed as Pliny was teaching him the French lyrics for songs he had in his head. On other occasions, though, he would reproach us quite severely for not taking his Pliny-conversations seriously.

Brighid and I had probably come across the name of Pliny somewhere among the classical elements in our education, but we would have been hard put to say anything definitive about him and certainly his name had no imaginative resonance for us. Still we read up about him in encyclopedias and discovered that there were two Plinys, Pliny the Elder and his nephew, the Younger Pliny, who wrote a famous letter describing the death of his uncle in the shadow of Vesuvius. Pliny the Elder seemed to have a massive appetite for study and research in the midst of a very busy life and there were amusing anecdotes about him such that he liked to use even his bath time for study by having people read to him while in the tub. For the sake of baiting Davoren, however, I pigeon-holed Pliny as an omnivorous cataloguer of facts, historical and scientific, and queried whether he would be a suitable soul-mate for an artistic religious explorer like himself.

Later on the cast of characters in Davoren's dialogues grew wider and more exotic. One scribbled record by Brighid on the subject of conversations in his head gives a sample of his richly-peopled imagination or interior life, however you want to categorise it. He wrote: "I had dialogues with great thinkers like Homer and Einstein, world explorers like Scott and Vasco da Gama, sensitive women like Lady Gregory and painters like Gauguin." Frankly, I never took these Pliny revelations or similar nuggets of wisdom he claimed to have received from other voices all that seriously in a literal sense. I am not attracted to tales of psychic powers or spooky phenomena, since I regard the ordinary activities of the human spirit as quite mysterious enough. Brighid however was more susceptible to taking psychic claims seriously and, in her painstaking, quarrying way, would endeavour to check out Davoren's references to the various historical figures whom he summoned up. For me they were clues to the kind of interior life he must have had for many years sitting in isolation in clinics, hospitals or care units or even at home. Even with the kind of back-up we provided for Davoren, the amount of time available for thinking when you are not capable of taking part in the normal childish interactions is enormous.

Yet as Davoren's output became more intriguing and challenging, I found I had to review my prejudices. And now, looking back on his singular journey in this world, I am forced to conclude that some of Davoren's intuitions were indeed uncanny, his 'tone of voice' at times compellingly authoritative and his insights deeply provoking. Overall, the incarnation of these powers in his young, frail and mostly helpless frame was unfailingly shocking.

Taking low-key intimate examples of his divining powers first, we and our friends were frequently disconcerted by his interventions in conversation from his letter-board around the dining-room table. To some degree he carried on his mother's role of match-maker, fixer and general prober of people's hearts but Davoren added a bluntness and directness that were not part of Brighid's repertoire. Some new friends that Brighid made when studying for her M. Ed. were so shaken by truths which Davoren uttered on first meeting them—referring to deep issues in their lives of which we would not have been aware—that they were not able for him, and walked away from the strong encounter with themselves which Davoren had provoked. On a slightly less serious note, Davoren regularly had fiery and frank exchanges with his godfather, Joe Dunne, a friend from my philosophy days. His poem 'Joe's Demons' gives a sample of the style of this good-humoured but searing banter:

> *Love's woes are wrestling*
> *with quests for autonomy;*
> *each demon struggles*
> *when both could sing in harmony.*

Davoren/Pliny putting himself/themselves forward as readers of people's hearts could largely be taken as part of the cheeky bravado which Davoren liked to exhibit, but it had a more profound significance when it came to Davoren's communication with his fellow-mute friends, other 'silent' ones. Over the years Davoren built up a very strong contact with three other children with very similar difficulties to his own, Siobhán Walsh from Kilkenny, who attended the Marino Clinic school in Bray for several years, James Brosnan, originally from Kerry, whom Davoren met at age four when they were both having hip operations in Cappagh Orthopaedic Hospital, and Stephen Olwill, a sparky redhead with a flair for music. Siobhán was a year or two older than Davoren, James his own age and Stephen a few years younger, but these age differences didn't seem to matter.

Nonetheless there was a chord of communion across the barriers between these kindred spirits. Sometimes it was silent co-presence with a transfixed look on Davoren's face. It would not be exactly a looking at each other, especially in Davoren's case, as in his chair he usually couldn't hold his gaze steadily in one direction. All four fellow-charioteers and warriors in disability had a very intense look, which could be loving, needy or fierce; these were (happily still are, in the case of Stephen, James and Siobhán) looks in which there is no dissimulation. They have no social gambits which enable them to hide their feelings and there is no hiding-place for the onlooker either (though Davoren could blank off very effectively when he wanted to). More often the communication between Davoren and his young friends was played out in agitated kicking, grimacing and grunting, the sheer vitality of which gave it a beauty all its own. Siobhán, James and Stephen have all developed more effective semi-independent signalling systems than Davoren ever did, nonetheless the bulk of their communication when they met was pre- or non-verbal. In Davoren's words, "we naturally become tuned to listening to hearts when we cease to move about." Thus his oft-expressed wish later in life to work as a counsellor with handicapped people may have seemed in the eyes of the world a preposterous notion but at a deeper level it made a certain sense.

With Siobhán Walsh, Davoren developed an intense boy-girl bond which persisted over the years, even though they met very infrequently and even though he was always throwing his heart at the steady stream of beautiful girls that flowed through his life. They corresponded quite regularly and in my experience of their times together, there existed a strong chemistry between them. Davoren often said that his dream was to be together with Siobhán and in my own heart I have no doubt that his feelings for her were genuine. One little poem which he wrote for her conveys this deep affection:

> *Sapling was straightened*
> *when it felt the warm sun*
> *of your love on its tender bark.*
> *Searing wind abated,*
> *growth began anew.*

The most provocative, almost insufferable, way in which Davoren revealed himself as possessing unfathomable depths was in his formulations about religion. Of course we may notionally accept the saying of Jesus about the need to become as little children, but that does not stop us in practice scorning the actual religious insights of children and young people, which can get right up our adult noses. Just to give a sample of the tone of some of his remarks, take these pronouncements about the painter Marc Chagall: "I love Chagall. I encountered Chagall in heaven shortly after he died. He captures my heart as no other painter does. We need Chagall to dream with, lest head rule heart. Religion guides his inspiration. Yiddish themes are rich in sexual imagery. Lovers feature in many such scenarios and Zaida the sacred goddess is depicted in many of the pictures where a sexual theme is at a quiescent and lyrically sensual level. Chagall explained a lot to me." We had in the house at the time a very finely-illustrated book on Chagall but Davoren would have been given a very cursory introduction to it.

On another occasion, after saying that listening to Handel's Messiah had made him melancholy, he went on: "Real faith in Christ depends on music because the music of the spheres is an example of God's presence." Just to counteract the whiff of pomposity and religiosity from these declarations, it is interesting to find on the same scrap of paper a vulgar childish reply to the question of what he would like to drink. "Lizard juice beer or snot cocktail" was his request.

There were regular oracular pronouncements such as "God is the weaver and religion, however warped, the multi-coloured warp." One I find particularly interesting is the following: "Coming to terms with God is impossible. God and I are on two separate planes of existence. I am surrounded by love. God is love. That's where our two worlds intersect." This may be considered a completely wrong-headed point of view but, like all potent formulations, it is deeply suggestive. Davoren also composed many little prayers, which often managed to combine reverence and cheeky playfulness. 'Sins of Little Scallywags' was the title of one which emphasised his impish nature while 'A Soft Little Prayer' leans towards awe and wonder:

O God our Father quite puissant,
grant us little people merry moments.
Show thy almighty splendour
in wondrous moments and light-filled days.

My mention of Jesus's espousal of little children should not mislead. Both Brighid and I were deeply opposed to Davoren being treated as a little Jesus explaining the scriptures or the 'meaning of life' to the doctors and priests even if at times the stage-set seemed to suggest such an interpretation. At heart all we wanted was for Davoren to be able to express himself and to find a pathway in life on which to meet up with friends and comrades and to challenge and love them and in turn be challenged and loved by them.

An insight by Sorcha Saidléar, who became a key helper with Davoren, shows that Davoren's own goal in life was not to be an untouchable revered enigma but to take his place in the cut-and-thrust of life. Sorcha told me that in their long free-ranging 'discussions,' Davoren used the character of Pliny for his explorations of God, for his attempts to fathom his handicap, his fears and his isolation, while teenage scallywaggery was expressed in his own 'voice'. However, as he moved into normal schooling and as he won friends and respect, Pliny receded, as if he had belonged to the dark, trapped side of Davoren's life while the boy (soon-to-be man) Davoren was trying to shimmy and soar towards life and light.

Happy Beaver in the Limelight

An unusual interview took place on Mike Murphy's midday radio programme in 1986 when Davoren was asked to review 'Mask' starring Cher, Sam Elliot and Eric Stolz. The film was about a teenage boy with a severe facial disfigurement, being brought up by his mother who was a wild biker and Hell's Angel enthusiast. Davoren wrote out some remarks beforehand but also attempted to make *ad lib* inserts, thrashing about on Brighid's lap during commercial and musical breaks, and while Mike chatted with Brighid. Part of his contribution went as follows:

> I want to do justice to a film about a handicapped boy by having it reviewed by a handicapped boy, not by bystanders who have only a skin-deep understanding of how it feels to be different. I know the heartbreak of loneliness and isolation excruciatingly felt in the marrow of my being. When gentle old ladies ask my care worker Audrey, "Does he understand me when I talk to him?" I want to roar polite curses in their faces. I do not blame them really. I blame a system of education that segregates normal children away from handicapped children so that we encounter each other as aliens.

Shortly after this polemical intervention, Davoren wrote: "Mike, I have too much to say and my Ma is telling me to belt up."

A personal and political battle against segregation and institutionalisation of handicapped people and for integration became a passionate obsession for the remainder of Brighid and Davoren's lives. Complex arguments for and against need not detain us here; suffice it to say that it was a shared dream which in many ways went beyond reason but one which had a radiant flowering in Davoren's life and circle of friends despite many ravages.

The first breakthrough towards integration occurred in 1987 when he was accepted as a pupil in sixth class in St Patrick's National School in Drumcondra. But like all the ascendant moments in Davoren's life, it was only possible because of the vision and energy of remarkable individuals, namely Eoin Shanahan and Sorcha Saidléar. The brightness which came into Davoren's world was fanned into life by these two intrepid spirits.

□□□□

Earlier in the spring of 1987, Angela Boushel, the "nurse of crisp perfection" and "passionate lover of justice" who had first come to our house as a schoolgirl when Davoren was only a baby, decided to go to Edinburgh. She wanted to break out of what she experienced as the strait-jacket of nursing and expand her horizons generally. But Angela was remarkably thoughtful and dedicated to our welfare and knew that Brighid needed an ally who would take inspiration and guidance from her, but who would in turn be a solid support and confidante for her in her anxieties and explorations about Davoren's future. So she went and found us Sorcha Saidléar, who was at the time doing relief work with St Michael's House Developmental Day Centre in Ballymun.

Thus the remarkable Saidléar family entered our lives. Daughter of Séamus Saidléar, an East-coast native Irish speaker, and Helmi, born in Germany but also Irish-speaking from childhood, Sorcha was the eldest of three girls. The youngest, Clíona, whom we have already met, became a very important 'sibling' a year or so after Sorcha's arrival, while the other sister, Róisín, was an honorary 'sibling' for parties and other celebrations. We will meet the elder son, Colm, in a later chapter. By degrees, the whole family became a huge support network for us, which continues to this day. The younger son, Eoin, must have wondered what was happening his family as various members migrated for considerable periods of time to Davoren Hanna's place.

Sorcha seemed right as a friend, helper and 'elder sister' for Davoren from the start. I cannot remember any dramatic moment when she began typing with him. Rather it seemed to happen quite naturally and, even more so than with Audrey, whom we met in the last chapter, they developed a style of easy chat which allowed Davoren to unburden himself of huge layers of normal concerns which the intense and poetically-charged bond with Brighid left somewhat in abeyance. Unlike Audrey, however, Sorcha generally kept no record of these chats. They were private and indeed instead of speaking out her contribution when they were talking, she would spell it out on the keyboard, steering Davoren to the letters as they silently gossiped, debated, giggled or learnt Irish.

With Sorcha on the scene, Brighid had one key element for the integrated schooling plan. There would be no point in Davoren going to normal school without a helper to work with him in the classroom and look after his feeding, toileting and medical needs. The local senior National School, St Patrick's in Drumcondra, under its principal John Blake, was willing to accept him. The missing link was the provision of funding for Sorcha. Brighid and Davoren went into political campaigning overdrive, lobbying TDs and the Department of Education. They were a formidable political force when roused and eventually a scheme was set up which enabled Sorcha to be paid for working with Davoren during the school year. The stage was set for his entry into 'normal' school.

□□□□

The main problem Eoin Shanahan, or 'Shano' as he quickly became affectionately known, had with accepting Davoren into his classroom was not Davoren himself, but this other adult figure, namely Sorcha, shadowing his daily performance. Fortunately, the trial sessions went splendidly and Davoren and Sorcha quickly settled down to being part of Shano's "busy happy beavers/ building mounds of knowledge/ and damming the streams of dark water/ where once I used to drown."

I remember vividly wheeling Davoren down the steps of our house for his first full day at real school. He was kicking manically with such force that his satchel fell off his lap. Rarely can a boy have set off for school with such glee. His delight was well justified because in St Pat's, he found an energetic hum of learning and creativity. I visited Shano's classroom

96

several times but my main evidence for the quality of his work is Davoren's reports and work-books. It was like being in the centre of an ordered whirlwind of activity. While Davoren had a little room in which Sorcha could attend to his needs, I think he needed to go there occasionally to recuperate from the brainstorm. I'm quite sure that Eoin always brought out the best of whatever class he was dealing with, but Davoren had additional good fortune in that the sixth class that year was an exceptionally bright and good-spirited one. All the usual high jinks and verbal sallies of boys of eleven or twelve were there but the energies were orchestrated beautifully.

'Poets' Corner' was a well-established 'Shano' institution before Davoren ever came on the scene and, even more than when in the company of fellow prize-winning young writers, he was able to relish being part of a shared activity as each week the palm of acclamation was passed around the class. After each weekly session there was a vote on which poem the lads liked best, and Davoren was the favourite no more frequently than anyone else. There was a great spirit of fairness and celebration of each other in the class, and through his friendship with Davoren, Pat Ingoldsby was invited along to adjudicate at one gathering in Poets' Corner.

I remember well one boy who specialised in writing poems with very long riddles as the titles; the poem itself then turned out to be a few words or phrases. He had a good sense of theatre and his teasing conundrums were especially popular. Then there were the clever rhyme specialists and those who flirted with risqué themes, mild enough mischief in most cases. Davoren would occasionally be found among these rhythmic rhymers and poetic pranksters, but often the 'poetic' voice which he had forged in isolation would betray him and words or phrases which he used would require an explanation. Davoren's first steps in poetry had been expressions of outrage and defiance at threats to his very survival; it was only later that he came to sing joyfully of conviviality and camaraderie. An example of this spirit of simple self-forgetful jubilation among his peers which found its way into Davoren's writing at that time is contained in a ballad he wrote about a football match. I quote just the last verse:

"Come on, Pat's, come on!"
— the tension mounted.
Slipping and sliding
in the treacherous slime,
the points eluded
the valiant team.
Goals were scored
but the prize went alas
to the brasher lads.
Yet the grins returned
to the Pat's boys' faces
when their loyal fans
cheered them off the field.

Other highlights of the school year were Irish and strangely art. The combined efforts of Eoin and Sorcha meant that Davoren caught up very substantially in Irish, which had been neglected up to then. The effect of this was that he was able to write several 'inventive' poems in Irish in later years when he went on to secondary school. Art flourished among Shano's beavers just as much as poetry and I remember well my visit to the school art display seeming like a washing and refreshment of the senses, such was the vitality of the work on show. The effect of this atmosphere on Davoren was to restimulate his old lunging efforts to make his mark on paper. He and Sorcha devised a way of working which meant he could make a contribution to the art display. For homework, he and Brighid did a lot of work rifling through art books and magazines at home in order to illustrate his writings and poems. All of this bore fruit again when he went on to secondary school; a teacher at Pobalscoil Rosmini, Margaret Keenan, worked with him very painstakingly and produced some very interesting effects.

❏❏❏❏

In an ironic reversal of the queries raised about him making his First Communion, it was Davoren himself who raised a storm about making his Confirmation. About two weeks before the ceremony, he wrote a letter to the chaplain saying that he had difficulty being confirmed because of the satanic element in man's nature, that death and destruction seemed to prevail over goodness and that he wanted to reflect on these matters before making a commitment. It seems that he was much exercised at the time by the Holocaust and a threatened revival of the arms race with the US 'Star Wars' proposals. He raised these queries at the time when the boys would have been scheduled to go to confession and perhaps have a chat before making their Confirmation. I don't recall exactly how this matter was resolved; all I can say is that he had that year in Sorcha and Eoin Shanahan two sincere and level-headed guides to help him through his difficulties. In the event, he made his Confirmation with his new-found pals. Moreover, some of his prayers that he had set to music were sung during the ceremony and he composed a beautiful poem, which has a powerful sting when you consider that, when he was in distress, each breath was literally a miracle for Davoren.

Sacred Spirit

You are each breath I take—
warm soft gulps of life's energy
filling my hungry heart.
No limp-feathered
wind-fearing dove
are you, my friend,
but a river of hope
in a dry season.
From your sacred banks
children drink wise adult years.

ㅁㅁㅁㅁ

Just as our Letterfrack Christmas marked the acme of Davoren's flourishing within the family circle, so his year in St Pat's was undoubtedly the period in which his zest for life as a normal child with friends and normal teenage interests had its greatest flowering. When he finished in St Pat's, he was thirteen. His public profile was growing all the time, his 'voice' was now more widely acknowledged. Of course all this public notice was important to him but the real source of his happiness at the time was the day-to-day interactions with his St Pat's classmates. For the first time in his life, he had a gang of friends of his own age to the house for his birthday party, he had outings and general gallivanting with his peers.

But there was always a shadow side to Davoren's life, as pain and torment were his nearly constant bed-fellows. The whole drama of his existence is neatly summed up in scraps of writing for which I don't have a precise date but which I know were written around that period. His conclusion was:

> The temptation to die is very strong at the moment. I lie awake all night coughing and I hear God saying, "Come to me, little boy, only don't feel sad. I will keep watch over your Mama and Dada." I must die however God decides. Real life starts after death, I assure you! I love you but I won't be able to stay much longer with you on earth. The long life story of Davoren Hanna is not to be. Please will you write my story. We will be famous.

While these declarations were shocking to us in their frankness, they were not surprising because we too lived through those nights of coughing and choking. Looking back at the Confirmation photographs, I am struck by how wan he looks and I recall that, in addition to it being a time of flourishing and fulfilment for him, it was also a wearying cycle of sleepless nights. After an evening spent working on homework with him, sorting out his psychodramas and either giving way to or squashing his desire to write a poem, Brighid would still have to face getting through the night, at best listening to the sound of distressed breathing, at worst taking turns with me in getting up to comfort him, change his position or drain his chest. If I was off for the evening, I would be a back-up service for Brighid and Davoren, preparing meals, washing dishes, making cups of tea or taking over when she collapsed from exhaustion. If I was working, she would if possible have a helper who would at least do some of the heavy work with Davoren, and, if she was lucky, be able to do some typing with him. When I came home around 11.30 or so, I would often have to take the helper or baby-sitter (as we sometimes still lapsed into calling them) home. Then we would settle down to have a little time for ourselves, to review the day's events, and to have our nightcap tea and toast. Often during this settling-down period, there would already have been several shattering disturbances — just as the tea was made, for instance — and our nerves would already be all-a-jangle when we eventually went to bed around one a.m. Then "for spite" (we could not help ourselves thinking and saying), just as we were about to settle ourselves, the real crescendo of distress would begin. Usually I would take the first shift, doing the physical things with him such as postural drainage and trying to clear the phlegm from the back of his throat which caused continual gagging, but also trying to sing, read or play music to him. But often I too would reach my limit and Brighid would have to take over again, or the two of us would stay up with him for a while in order to sustain each other. This pattern often went on until about four in the morning. Fortunately, we usually took it in turns to reach our respective breaking points. If one of us was run ragged for a week or so, the other would keep a balancing levity. The real turn of the screw in these middle-of-the-night encounters with fear and abject helplessness was that we knew that Davoren also knew it was a terrible fate and he knew that we knew it was a pitiless grind. It was a crazy, killing way of life and we knew it but we couldn't see any way out.

Early morning often bade fair to be the cruellest cut of all. We would struggle out of the bed about 7.30 to get him ready for school — to find him in a deep peaceful sleep. Ravaged at the prospect of waking him, we'd feel heartless. Then a remarkable thing would happen: when we woke him, he would smile at us seraphically. Our standard joke at the time was that he emitted a dangerous radiation and we often fell down or had to shield ourselves from the splendour of his smile. All this jocosity only served to brighten his countenance even more and temporarily the horrors of the night would be forgotten. His resilience (not always) after these racking, sleepless nights was truly staggering. I occasionally had a bad bout of coughing or choking when something I was eating went down the wrong way, for example, leaving me shaken and exhausted. This kind of rending of his whole body was however a day-and-night companion to Davoren, and yet he surfaced for long periods each day with a captivating radiance.

Many of these rhythms of fatigue and endurance, of despair and buoyancy will be familiar to parents of young children going through a difficult patch, but with us it had now gone on for thirteen years, even as we were entering into a deeper and deeper commitment to keep Davoren at home until we could open up an arena of flourishing for him. Whatever may have been the likelihood when he was younger of abandoning him into the care of others (institutional care if you like), while somehow maintaining a parental bond with him, the idea of such a release from the grinding home-routine now seemed unthinkable. Yet a time-bomb of chronic strain and exhaustion was building up in our midst.

□.□□□

Brighid had no master plan (or as she might put it in her iconoclastic feminist moods, no mistress plan) to help all three of us make our way through the narrow gate of survival with a modicum of dignity. She lived too much in the eye of the storm to develop such a comprehensive blueprint. Nevertheless, she was constantly thinking, improvising and scheming and in retrospect I can see a deep pre-vision underlying the arrangements for our lives that she began to set in place around that time.

Even as the network of helpers that later became known as the 'siblings' was beginning to form around him, it was clear that we couldn't manage Davoren at home on our own. He required twenty-four-hour one-to-one back-up, and the pressure on Brighid, in particular, was intolerable. Far from the psychological umbilical cord slackening, she was becoming a reluctant Siamese twin to Davoren, her world being sucked almost without residue into Davoren's. Brighid very rarely took to the bed with sickness but her health was a nagging, underlying worry. Many close friends of hers tried to tell her that she was putting her physical and psychological health at risk; some indeed found the stranglehold in which she seemed to have locked herself too painful to observe and so walked away.

An early episode (recounted to me many years later by Clíona) in the expansion of the siblings illustrates very well the chaotic life rhythm which was engulfing us. Sorcha Saidléar had introduced Clíona to our circle and she in turn brought her close friend Helena Boyd into the fold.

In advance of Helena's first visit, Clíona was telling her what she could expect:

> Don't be put off by Brighid. She's a powerful presence and can be a bit explosive, especially at mealtimes. The diabetes causes her to get a bit agitated. Sometimes she gets dopey when she's trying to eat her dinner and sometimes she gets aggressive and can swear like a trooper. But it'll pass and you'll have great fun with her.

This was a true enough picture during a certain period. Brighid was making the transition from insulin derived from pigs to synthetically-reproduced human insulin and could be a bit unstable. Her speech would get slurred and she would appear as if she were drunk. In the meantime, the helper would be trying to get on with the job of feeding Davoren, usually an hour-and-a-half exercise. As for myself, Clíona told Helena:

> You don't have to worry about Jack. He'll be out in the kitchen (a poky little hole at the time) clattering with pots and pans, washing up and preparing meals. He'll be listening to the news on his earphones (intravenous news, Brighid used to call it). Then he goes off to work. For all practical purposes, you can forget about him.

> As for Davoren, he's just himself. Difficult at times but a charmer.

This affectionate picture of shambling domesticity belied the fact that our financial resources were becoming very seriously depleted. We had started off paying Davoren's baby-sitters in the normal way, increasing the rate as the years went by. Even though the role had developed and the people working with him weren't doing it primarily for the money, we continued to try to pay the going rate. Brighid was too concerned for the welfare of anyone who came into the house not to insist on them getting a fair return for their support for us. There were all kinds of additional costs associated with Davoren — a problem which health board cuts on the supply of nappies brought to a head. For a time, Davoren and Brighid's energies were diverted into political campaigning to have the full quota restored. Stinging letters were sent off to Charlie Haughey and to Bertie Ahern, whom we had met at the Stephen Roche 'Freeman of Dublin' celebrations, and there were plans afoot to join with other parents in dumping wet nappies outside the Dail. Bertie, to his credit, took Dav's political outspokenness in his stride and, even though we were never Fianna Fail supporters, went out of his way to open any door that he could for Davoren. They later became occasional drinking companions in Bertie's local, Davoren with his gang of young friends and Bertie with the local FF workers.

At that time of mounting strain, Pat Ingoldsby was an occasional visitor to the house. Now Pat may play the court jester in public, having adopted a persona of marvel and delight at life's quixotic revelations, but he is a very intelligent man who is no stranger to the darker side of life with its struggles against misfortune, as Davoren's poem 'Dark' testifies — "you sacrificed your savage pain/ to huckleberry your life away." Pat, on his own initiative, spoke to his RTÉ colleague, author and journalist June Levine, about the pressures threatening the eclipse of this young talent and the collapse of an entire family. Pat and June's desks adjoined one another in RTÉ at the time but, beyond that happy coincidence, Pat knew his woman when he approached June for help. After some initial resistance, she was hooked by Davoren's plight and pluck. Being the resourceful, determined and compassionate woman that she is, she immediately set to work on two fronts: one, fund-raising and two, publicity. June didn't waste her energies getting sucked into the maelstrom of our household (she probably realised that one strong woman operating in that arena was quite sufficient). Rather she knew that she could help best by working at a distance, detached from the day-to-day turmoil of Davoren's life.

She got Brighid to itemise the financial requirements to enable him to complete his second-level schooling, while continuing to live at home; this was about as far as we were thinking at the time. She also wanted Brighid to set out the minimum requirements to transform the house into which we had moved just as we were discovering that Davoren was handicapped. Davoren's bedroom had taken over the front downstairs room and all the rest of the household activity — feeding, toileting, communicating, physical care, exercise — took place in one small room. It was a wonderfully intense and dynamic room but like a dangerously over-charged pressure chamber. Literally so, as the whole house needed to be rewired. The final item on her list was the resources needed to research and solve his communication problems.

June's other campaign front was the media. June had been a pioneering researcher with 'The Late, Late Show' for many years and was working with 'Kenny Live' when we first met her, although she was gradually withdrawing from that role to concentrate on her independent writing. Still she investigated all the issues connected with Davoren and set up an appearance on 'Kenny Live'.

Brendan Kennelly and Brighid made the case that evening to the viewers that a unique voice would be silenced unless help was forthcoming. Davoren and I sat in the front row of the studio audience, both very tense, but in Brighid and Brendan we had two very powerful advocates. Pat Kenny was himself very impressed by Davoren's work. Writing about Brighid in the home setting, I sometimes paint her as a turbulent colourful larger-than-life character and that she was. Some of these 'gestures' of her personality were like a last throw of the dice in her battle for survival and sanity in the midst of her own health problems and the mesmerising burden of Davoren. Yet in her true nature, she was a deeply thoughtful, sensitive and articulate woman with a balancing leaven of humour. All of this came across very powerfully in the interview. Brendan, who must be counted as one of the great encouragers in Irish life, was passionate and serious in presenting his view of Davoren, while emphasising the puckish humour which permeated his vision.

All manner of initiatives flowed from the 'Kenny Live' appearance. June set up a properly-constituted fund (with trustees Ivor Browne, Mary

Finan and Adam Mesbur), Woodie's DIY committed themselves to building a suitable extension for Davoren, for which Pat Kenny's architect brother, Frank, kindly offered to do the design, and offers of technological help and expertise flowed in. We did some work with Paddy Matthews from the School of Engineering in UCD and Jim Davenport, who worked in the Children's Hospital in Crumlin (both contributed ingenuity and a strong personal touch with Davoren) but we eventually settled on a systematic effort to break the code of Davoren's communication with Dr David Vernon from the School of Computer Science in Trinity College.

Having spent time in the computer industry by the time we met him, David had already achieved high distinction in academic research. At one level he was like a grown-up version of the 'eager beavers' of Davoren's school poems: full of the intense and wide-ranging curiosity of the scientist and the action-man 'can-do' mentality of the engineer. He had that indefatigable spirit so necessary in any true innovator of being willing to patiently explore all possible variations of a plausible solution; but, if that approach proved fruitless, he would start all over again with a new hypothesis. In between meetings with us, he sent us regular progress reports on the acquisition of pieces of equipment and the checking of parallel research.

In addition to all these methodical, orderly and intellectual qualities, mirrored so well in his neatly-trimmed moustache, bright eyes and rapid economical movements, David was deeply aware of the psychological whirlpool into which he was attempting to make a helpful intervention. More than that, he had immense respect, even reverence, for the intuitive understanding between Davoren and Brighid and the other communication helpers. Davoren called David a wizard and numbered him among his inventive saviours, but this was very far from how David saw himself.

David had already done some research on tracking eye movement, using a camera interpreted by a computer, which seemed a very promising approach to explore with Davoren. We already used an informal version of this approach to get a 'yes' or 'no' answer from him, although it did depend on him being in a suitably relaxed posture to begin with. If Davoren could establish a consistent control of his eye movements, he could make selections among groups of letters and eventually write and communicate independently. In theory, a speech-box could be incorporated into the system. In practice, many people with significant handicaps are 'voiced' in this way.

Many permutations of this eye-tracking were tried, ranging from fitting Davoren with a helmet to which a camera was attached, to scanning him from a distance. The efforts of Brighid and myself and the various helpers were channelled into setting Davoren up for these sessions and recording the results. Davoren invented the title 'Diary of a Gong-Ringer' for one notebook recording these experiments. Because of the huge load which Brighid was already carrying, and because of my own very intermittent success at the lap communication, I played an important role in these trials.

In practice, the work never went smoothly. Davoren always showed initial promise and enthusiasm for any new approach we tried, but then his ability to control his eye movements would desert him. I and other helpers often got impatient with him, and that didn't help matters very much. But our anger and impatience were really beside the point. To anyone who had clear eyes to see, there was always some intrusive element in Davoren's contorted body contributing to the breakdown. He would have a major or minor seizure or he would slide to one side and not be able to re-adjust himself. We liaised a lot with the Occupational Therapy Department in the CRC about different kinds of seating for Davoren and received great support from Andrew Semple and his staff but there was no seating available which met the full spectrum of seating needs of someone who was so significantly disabled.

Brighid's image for what Davoren needed — "a mechanical lap" — seemed more apt than ever but even more elusive. My own phrase in a poem I had written several years earlier was "fertile museful lap', which drew attention to the lap as responsive to Davoren's body, drawing him back when he fell too far (off the typewriter keyboard, for instance), but also to the fact that Davoren's communicativeness had been nurtured on and had never really moved away from this intimate form of human contact.

Over the nearly ten years, starting from his early communication efforts, during which we tried to harness Davoren to technology, we would often call to mind his preference for "soft boobs" rather than "hard-edged switches" as a springboard for his writing. We would recall this phrase mostly in fun, but sometimes in screaming anger and frustration. In our hearts I think we did feel that there was a reluctance in him to grow up, despite his adult-like utterances.

But then when he suffered wrenching convulsions, raw croaking chestiness, inflamed stomach ulcers and excruciating cramps, and when the only way to relieve his distress (apart from dosing him with analgesics) was to hold and hug him, to comfort him on the lap, to wrap our arms around his chest, to nuzzle and cradle him, then we understood too the distance he had already travelled and his possible reluctance to break away from that enfolding. Soon there would be even more reason to comfort and console him *and* to cajole and challenge him into maturity.

Autumn Auguries

Leaves whisper soft messages
of farewell in my fascinated ear;
lapfuls of mossy chestnuts are stored
in nature's bountiful cupboard;
the little mimicking music-birds
pause in wonder as the heavens
shed their russet and ochre tears.

This early little poem that Davoren wrote for his mother was called 'Autumn Concerto'. During the months of September to November in 1988, Davoren must have felt a sustained upsurge in the concerto of his life. At the beginning of September he started second-level education in Pobalscoil Rosmini, a local community school. A few weeks later he was off to Wales to receive an award and then in November he was in London again, this time to receive second prize in his age-category in a major competition organised by *The Observer* newspaper.

Even after the heady, overwhelmingly positive year in St Pat's, the move to Rosmini was not the least of these autumn events in Davoren's estimation. Rather it was a whole new stage in his integration into the normal channels of life. Paradoxically, as the severity of Davoren's disability was pushing us beyond normal limits in coping and finding resources, his entry into normal schooling and activities was being facilitated by a group of extraordinary ordinary people.

The actual administrative transfer of Davoren to Rosmini was very straightforward in comparison with some of our earlier battles. Rosmini was already home to several blind and partially-sighted boys moving on from St Joseph's School run by the Rosminian order. They had never had anyone like Davoren but the overall spirit we encountered was one of

109

"we'll give it a go". Bride Rosney, now an adviser to President Robinson, was principal at the time. In general the school considered it an honour and a challenge to adapt to someone like Davoren. Again a small room was provided for his needs — it quickly became known as Dav's Den — but otherwise he received no special treatment.

Secondary school with its longer school day, continual transfer between classes and a whole range of teachers having to adjust to Davoren and his helper, was much more daunting than primary school. Fortunately Sorcha Saidléar agreed to ease the transition by continuing on for a month while she was waiting for her nursing training to commence. Sorcha had been a human dynamo in her commitment to the job, which was going to make her a hard act to follow. Fortunately, as so often in Davoren's life, at times of greatest stress, someone (in this case, unusually, a young man) came along to meet the need.

Gary Rutherford was large, voluble and boisterous. He had done a considerable amount of building work in his time and had the physique and the 'no problem' lash-into-it attitude to match. You could imagine him as the man to call on for a demolish-and-rebuild mission. Gary had been coming to our house one evening a week for about a year-and-a-half, while doing a Social Studies Course in Cathal Brugha Street. As he says himself, his first impression, after he had been coaxed by a class colleague to come up to our house and had seen the relatively comfortable houses in the neighbourhood, was: "These are just a couple of richies who want to dump their kid on someone."

Gary didn't find 'richies' but he did find a house full of books and chat which intimidated him on the first night, and left his head buzzing. There was a big crowd that evening, with Dav's godfather, Joe Dunne, and Cian and Annette visiting. Yet Gary soon learned to relax in the home atmosphere which was a cross between a philosophy and literature seminar, a therapy room and a railway station. He found his own witty, vivid, distinctive story-telling voice, which was to have a heartbreaking consummation in laughter and tears around Davoren's coffin many years later. But he also found a voice in which to express honest insight, confusion and angry frustration, sometimes with Davoren and sometimes with those who so blatantly misunderstood and mistreated him. Gary stayed to work with Davoren over several years. "But it wasn't like work" — it was a passion and a torment that turned Gary's world upside down.

Gary joined Dav and myself on a trip up to the Phoenix Park for a fireworks display during the Millennium Year. Being ultra-wary of getting stuck in a traffic jam, I left the car miles away and we pushed Davoren across the fields in the Park for three-quarters-of-an-hour to get a good vantage-point. "We froze the arse off him," Gary recalls, and then adds: "I had to sit at home with him for hours with his feet under my pullover, trying to warm them up." Davoren's poor circulation and lack of exercise left him extremely vulnerable to cold feet. Gary also remembers playing "mammies and daddies" with Sorcha while Brighid and I were away for a few days and the holy terror which paralysed them if they got something wrong in Davoren's routine.

At that point in September 1988 Gary was working in upstate New York, with an option to stay on for a year, when Brighid rang to say that she would like him to take over the school job with Davoren. He says she put no moral pressure on him, but within an hour "Helper Bear" (a phrase he had coined when Mammy Bear, Daddy Bear, Davoren Bear and he were on a visit to the CRC) was on his way back to Ireland.

Over the next year, Davoren brought Gary to the edge — "to the end of my limits" — as he failed over several months to communicate with Davoren at the letter-board and felt useless with him in the classroom. Davoren's fondness for women helpers and friends, apart from his school pals, was a big theme at the time — Cian used to tease him mercilessly about his flock of females — and this led Gary to doubt himself, "It's because I don't have tits."

Another dangerous limit was reached on an occasion when Brighid miscalculated and sent Davoren away on his own with Gary for several days in the company of another family to the Aran Islands. The other family didn't really know Davoren well so Gary ended up having to do nearly all the work, coping also with Davoren's night-time distress. "It was lucky there wasn't someone thrown over the cliffs at Dun Aengus," says Gary. In fact, Gary did everything to make Davoren's trip memorable, even constructing a hammock to carry him up to Dun Aengus, but he wore himself to the bone in the process. "It was the last time Brighid ever sent only one person away with Davoren," concludes Gary.

The break-up of the communication log-jam, when it came, had a suitably Gary-lous tone. On the brink of giving up, he decided one day to try one last time as both he and Dav were in a relaxed mood. Gary's heart jumped when he noted that Davoren was indicating clearly on the keyboard, but delight turned to dismay when he couldn't make a word out of the letters he was forming. "LEAQ," Davoren was typing. In the end, he was so determined, Gary let him go ahead and just type whatever he wanted. It turned out to be a poem called 'Loquacious Love', which attempted to explore the difficulties the two of them were having in the midst of their strong bond:

> Love sways;
> leaden Gary anchors me down,
> ranting leads to nothing
> but inactivity.
> As demons banish
> all goodness from hearts,
> the greatest deed
> of a sad feeble boy
> will be to lead
> a really great pal.

Gary was furious with Davoren for initiating communication with him by using a word "which I didn't even know the meaning of". And Davoren was too harsh. Gary was far from leaden and even if Gary was never one to forego a good old rant if the occasion demanded it, over time he and Davoren developed a heart-warming and heart-scouring dancing rhythm in the repartee between them.

But Davoren's capacity to find a path in normal schooling was never just dependent on a simple partnership. Thus Rosmini only became a sheltering and intellectually nourishing haven for Davoren because he found there teachers who took him in and engaged with him straightforwardly, if such a word could ever be appropriate for someone so crookedly decanted into the world.

Barry Gleeson, his English teacher during his five years at Rosmini, gave Davoren an excellent grounding in literature during classes, but, in addition, he became a mentor for his writing whom Davoren, and indeed Brighid and myself, respected enormously. Barry, a gifted singer of unaccompanied song, with a strong, robust voice, has himself a great passion for literature and writing and, insofar as he could, tried to stretch Dav. He lent him tapes of plays and poetry to listen to in the Den when Davoren had free classes. Ever the soul of discretion, Barry maintained a link with Davoren and his circle right to the end.

Through his spirited connection with the Saidléar family, and through his year with Shano, Davoren had learnt more Irish in a year or two than many children learn over years of schooling. Happily, this ardent bond was further fostered at Rosmini through his teacher Niamh Digan. Since teaching Irish to a gang of lads, some of whom are not particularly academic, is an uphill task at the best of times, Niamh had to adopt a firm, assertive style in the classroom, but outside the classroom, and in our home, Niamh was warm, teasing and playful with Davoren. Since Davoren's time and energy were limited, as was the energy of his helpers, he did very little work of any sort in Irish but he did eventually reward Niamh by writing a few poems in Irish. A simple, early one exploited his Irish vocabulary to the maximum with *lámha hata* being invented as an Irish word for handicap. Another poem in Irish, 'File beag,' echoes back to his very early poem, 'A Little Sound,' but has also a prophetic ring with its concluding line about "resurrection without death".

> *File beag greannmhar*
> *gan focal a rá*
> *—sin mise.*

> *Teach gan doras dúnta,*
> *tinn gan tinneas,*
> *aiséirí gan bás*
> *—sin mise.*

(A small funny poet without a word to say — that's me. A house without a closed door, ill without being in pain, resurrection without death — that's me.)

Even though teachers tried to treat him normally, inevitably Davoren's vulnerability and regular crises shattered the illusion. I remember well Niamh worrying — after Davoren had a major seizure in class and then was sick for several days — that her sharpness with the class, him included, might have upset him. In spite of Niamh's sensitivity, Davoren managed one of his major triumphs with her, when he was given detention for talking in class. Together with Gary, Davoren had been chatting at the back of the class with some of the pals. They were told to stop, which the others did. But Davoren kept acting agitated on Gary's lap, and so Gary let him type on. When Niamh came down and found Davoren trying to revive the interrupted conversation, she intervened.

Unfortunately, as the years went on and his communication problems intensified, his stamina for the school day and his ability to take a meaningful part in class activities deteriorated. Nevertheless Rosmini remained for his five years there an anchorage of stimulation and acceptance, a stronghold of challenge and integration.

Much of Davoren's development was topsy-turvy. He had to scale enormous peaks of maturation at a very early age in a way which suppressed huge reservoirs of the child in him. A lot of Davoren's schooling was as much a stepping back as a development; he had to learn to socialise and to adjust to the give-and-take of a group of tough and forthright boys. He was terribly used to the spotlight of attention at home and the special care of institutions dealing with handicapped people. Some of Davoren's relish in this new role comes out in a poem written when he was in '3G' in Rosmini. 'The Ronald Reagan Home for Senile Teachers' imagines the teachers looking back in their dotage on the horrors of '3G':

> *There they sit stupefied*
> *at prim terraced house windows*
> *watching their former pupils*
> *drive by in snazzy cars.*

Such premature senility
legendary Methuselah never
had to undertake to reach
his ancient toll-bridged years.
Frenzied old ladies beg for mercy
as they relive memories of '3G'
turning them on their roasting spit.
Spoiled exam papers stuff their greying heads
and when they eat hunger disappears
as they remember those suffering innocents
they've tortured over all the years.

□□□□

The ferry trip to Holyhead and the long drive down the length of Wales, past the forbidding peaks of Snowdonia, to Cardiff for the Awards ceremony gave us plenty of time to reflect on the purpose of all these literary jaunts. I for one was becoming heartily tired of them, though I could see that these boosts to his morale played a part in redeeming his life from the Sisyphean futility of ceaseless struggle, his daily battle for survival, literally to get enough food into his stomach for nourishment. Looking back with the wisdom of hindsight on Brighid's motivation, my sense is that she had an underlying awareness that time was running out for her and that she was desperate to put Davoren on some secure footing. My fear was that the work which would really consolidate Davoren's future, namely, developing independent communication and publishing a book of his poems or, alternatively, a book about his writing, was being neglected in the flurry of gallivanting.

As had happened so often before, all my anxiety and crankiness were assuaged by the hospitality and festivity surrounding the presentation of the Welsh Academy's Young Writers' Award to Davoren. Again we met a judge and writer, Hilary Llewellyn Williams, who was genuinely struck by the power of Davoren's writing — someone who saw through his disability to the original spark within. The prize-winning poem was his 'How-the-Earth-Was-Formed Quiz' with its startling images of "heaven's master-baker, lord of holocaust and light', of Pliny's reckless curiosity about the effects of the eruption of Vesuvius, and of swallows tuning into the earth's magnetic polarity. Several other poems by Davoren had been circulated among panels of artists associated with the Cardiff Literature Festival and a graphic artist, New York-born Paul Peter Piech, was so inspired by them he did lino-cut posters illustrating three of the poems. Mr Piech was one of that rare species nowadays, an illustrator and artist in the tradition of William Morris with a strongly humanist political credo.

Deciding to take the Fishguard-Rosslare route on our return journey, we drove in relentless blinding rain on wind-swept congested motorways to Fishguard, only to be told that the sailing was delayed for several hours. We were reasonably confident about Davoren's sea-legs as he had survived a rough passage on a scout-trip to the Isle of Man without misadventures but unfortunately our optimism was misplaced. He was very sick on the crossing, Brighid and Sorcha were knocked out with very queasy stomachs and we were collectively shattered by the time we set foot again on Irish soil. In the end, Wales was a revitalising if exhausting adventure.

❐❐❐❐

The theme of *The Observer* National Children's Poetry Competition in 1988 was 'Friends', so Davoren didn't have to write any special poems for the occasion, since it was already one of his big themes. Among over 41,000 entrants for the competition, he won second-prize in his age category for a poem he had written for his friend, Brian Coffey. Brian played the clarinet and Davoren compared his own "folded fists" measuring out a tune with Brian's "silver-fingered music-making". Among the prestigious members of the panel of judges was Ted Hughes, whose poetry Brighid would have introduced to Davoren. As well as having an almost mythical aura within the world of poetry, Ted Hughes is physically very striking — tall and broad, with a red weather-beaten face, slightly dishevelled hair and intense hooded eyes. Before presenting the prizes, he spoke quietly but eloquently about learning poetry 'by heart' and about steeping yourself in language-worlds, giving in his own case examples such as various books of the Bible and classical poets. I thought of the intensity of Davoren's immersion, not so much in books as in the *sruthanna* of language that surrounded him at home.

In a shy, awed encounter afterwards, Davoren and Ted Hughes met and from that meeting flowed his poem 'Two Foxy Scribes':

> *Silver-silent I—*
> *golden-tailed you—*
> *we both tell time-riddles.*
>
> *Limping across*
> *snow-scarred moonscapes,*
> *the spheres tumble at our bark.*

⊐⊐⊐⊐

Like Eliza Doolittle, Brighid would often protest, "I'm no lady." She translated the notion of refinement as 'sieved,' all lumps removed, denatured. To which I would often reply: "Methinks the lady doth protest too much." In fact, Brighid was a highly cultivated and cultured woman with great discernment in music and literature, with a gentle and beautiful speaking voice when in repose (but which sometimes betrayed an underlying sadness) and an acute sensitivity to the effects of any of her actions on others. But her shrieks of protest at the notion of being thought ladylike revealed a certain honest and truthful self-appraisal. Brighid was passionate, fiery and explosive; she didn't hide her emotions of delight or distress. As a teacher and nurturing mother, she could playfully orchestrate all that emotional energy into a creative rhythm, but in the stress and strain of daily living, restraint in expressing herself was not Brighid's trademark. I have already mentioned a certain instability and volatility which severe fluctuations in her blood sugar levels caused occasionally. Many of these characteristics of his mother are captured in a poem by Davoren called 'Friday Nights in Our Place (or Mother's Night Out)'. You can imagine for yourself her sentiments as she worked on it with him.

Grumpy mother drinks her cold tea
complaining all the while.
Hitting her head off the frescoed ceiling,
she swears vigorously,
then gives me a friendly cuff
before stomping out the door
dressed like some frantic half-wit.
Seconds later, the doorbell rings.
"I forgot to kiss you goodnight,"
she feverishly whispers.
Then her guilt satisfied,
she trundles down the steps
leaving me to Anna's calm arms.

The calm and quick-witted Anna Brady helped out evenings before becoming the successor to Gary in the school job with Davoren. In contrast to the effusive drama of Gary's interactions with Davoren, Anna brought a style of quiet, intimate and humorous conspiracy. She soldiered in Rosmini during a tougher period, with a higher level of teenage turbulence manifesting itself among the lads, Davoren included. The difficult role of being an adult figure sitting within a class of full-blooded youths was one on which each of the helpers had to stamp their own authority. While Gary's aura was strong and assertive, Anna's participation in this novel educational experiment was unobtrusive but equally effective, as Anna's composure commanded respect.

This equanimity made her a perfect foil for Brighid, whose sense of crisis was steadily intensifying. Behind the stage-manager role which she played in the household, Brighid's involvement with the siblings was subtle and complex. On the one hand, she was mother, advisor, confidante, elder sister, inspirational figure and role model. With some of the young men in particular, the influence she had as mother and confidante was poignant when it was not comical. Nevertheless, there was something absolutely authentic about this quality in her which drew people in. She was so unabashedly and nakedly herself that she gave people, particularly young people, liberty to be fully themselves in her company.

Giddy Rapture: Davoren at age two with Brighid and Jack
in the back garden of Bantry Road.

Nature Study: Davoren at age three in his back garden.

Jumpy Together: Brighid and Davoren, age four.

Shared Triumph: Davoren with his friend Mary Munnelly at the presentation of the Irish Schools Creative Writing Awards in 1985.

Folded Fist: Davoren and Jack trying to work at the
typewriter in 1986.

School Pals: Davoren with classmates from St Patrick's National
School, Drumcondra, in 1988: (from left) Mark Grange,
Dylan Owens, Paul Clonan, Paul Coffey and Martin Whatley.

Creative Platform:
Davoren with his parents
by the typewriter on the
living-room table in 1988.

Reading Pleasures:
Davoren with his father
Jack in early 1990.

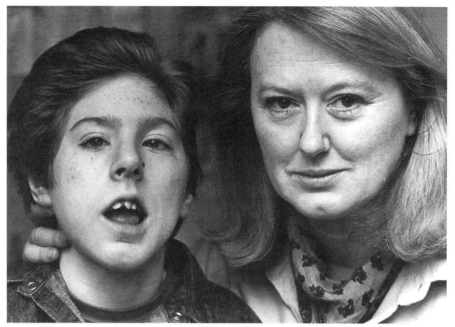
Fighting Spirits: Davoren with his mother Brighid in the spring of 1990.

Uncommon Rascals: Davoren with Brendan Kennelly at the launch of **Not Common Speech** in Waterstone's on 27th March 1990.

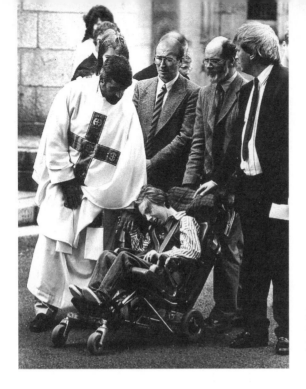

Healing Hand: Davoren with Fr Dara Molloy at his mother's funeral on 11th July 1990.

Smiling Siblings: Davoren is '98FM Dubliner of the Month' in November 1990. From left, back: Martyn Mulhere, Sorcha Saidléar, Helena Boyd, Jack Hanna, Eoin O'Byrne and Jane Voison. Front: Jim Lacey of National Irish Bank and Jeff O'Brien of 98FM.

Roguish Chuckles:
Davoren with John B Keane at
the People of the Year ceremony
at the Burlington Hotel in
November 1990.

Evening Farewell: Davoren leaving the party in the Trinity Bar to launch Barry
Gleeson's CD 'Path across the Ocean' on Friday, 15th July 1994.
Front: Martyn Mulhere, Davoren and Margaret Gleeson. Back: Jack Hanna,
Barry Gleeson and Mick O'Keeffe.

Final Journey: Davoren's father, Jack, places a rose on Davoren's coffin on 20th July 1994.

Poems Keepsake: A half-serious, half-joking will made by Davoren around 1985.

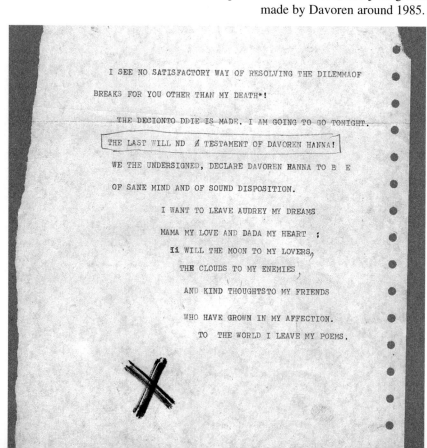

I SEE NO SATISFACTORY WAY OF RESOLVING THE DILEMMAOF

BREAKS FOR YOU OTHER THAN MY DEATH*!

THE DECIONTO DDIE IS MADE. I AM GOING TO GO TONIGHT.

THE LAST WILL ND Ø TESTAMENT OF DAVOREN HANNA!

WE THE UNDERSIGNED, DECLARE DAVOREN HANNA TO B E

OF SANE MIND AND OF SOUND DISPOSITION.

I WANT TO LEAVE AUDREY MY DREAMS

MAMA MY LOVE AND DADA MY HEART ;

I1 WILL THE MOON TO MY LOVERS,

THE CLOUDS TO MY ENEMIES

AND KIND THOUGHTSTO MY FRIENDS

WHO HAVE GROWN IN MY AFFECTION.

TO THE WORLD I LEAVE MY POEMS.

The other side of the picture was that Brighid needed a lot of mothering (and fathering) herself. This need was not a late emergence in her, a function of the rending of her heart over Davoren's painful struggles. During the first few months I knew her, she was mourning a school friend who had been an air hostess on the Aer Lingus plane which disappeared in the mysterious Tuskar Rock incident in 1968. Already there was something of an orphan about her, and as first her mother (1968) and then her father (1974) died, this feeling I had about her intensified, such that I wrote a poem for her called 'Orphan Wife'. While there was nothing pathological about it, she was continually in search of mother-figures and father-figures. She had a combative relationship with my father and, while she loved my mother, by the time Davoren was born my mother had become frail and worn.

Thus with the Angelas, Sorchas and Annas among the siblings, Brighid found a quasi-mothering. This female solidarity and nurture across the generations was a beautiful sight to behold. She had of course friends of her own age who were a great support, but in her later years the day-to-day care from bonding with the siblings was woven into the daily texture of her life.

The terrors of the nights with Davoren often drove Brighid into inassuageable aloneness. Often there was very little I could do to console her. No wonder that, like the psalmist, she cried out to a God whom she could not see, whom she felt had abandoned her. There were nights when I was chilled to the marrow as I witnessed the bleakness which took hold of her as Davoren's cries from downstairs stabbed our hearts. As well as these deep-seated psychological needs, there was the ongoing issue of her diabetes. While Brighid had never let her diabetes cast her in the role of a dependent person, she in fact needed a lot more taking care of than she was getting, or looked likely to be able to get.

Spring Sapling Keepsake

Serious work on publishing a selection of Davoren's poems only began in 1988, gathering momentum in 1989. The tardiness was due to exhaustion from our years of carrying the load and a certain amount of vacillation about what sort of book we ought to aim for. After much dithering, I decided that a book about Davoren's communication breakthrough and battles for acceptance was premature. In addition, my closeness to the story was at that time more of a hindrance than a help; I was too riven by conflict and frustration to be able to see and write clearly. There were technical hitches too in that Brighid was an atrocious typist and I was always behind in typing out good copies of poems from the rough scribbles and chaotically typed-out drafts. Even though we were awash with computers to explore Davoren's communication, there was no space with all his equipment to set up a simple table for printing out his poems.

We had met novelist and playwright Dermot Bolger at various poetry readings and literary events and his Raven Arts Press was very keen to publish Davoren's poems. Dermot was at all times hospitable to the project but never put any pressure on us. A bonus was that he was a local, living just down the road from us in Drumcondra. Meanwhile Brendan Kennelly and Barry Gleeson read through preliminary selections we made among Davoren's large output. We eventually decided to go for a small selection of his more crafted poems rather than a larger collection which would show many more quirky and bizarre sides to his writing, but which would put the spotlight more on Davoren as a handicapped writer. Dermot wanted to see Davoren in print as a writer first and foremost.

The records show that Davoren had a direct hand in choosing the daffodil yellow colour for the cover of the book and the photo of himself with the impish grin. He mainly rose to the occasion, however, by writing a highly distinctive preface, 'Notes from A Bone Fragment — Fleshed out with Poems'. When Brighid spoke in interviews of helping Davoren to fulfil his dreams "even if it kills me", it must have been periods like those spent working with Dav on that preface which led her to use such a dramatic expression. When I look at the zig-zagged pages full of cross-outs and stabs at interpreting his unusual turns-of-phrase, I can almost literally feel the strain on her back and arms, the liftings and wipings, the interruptions for coughing and choking sessions and seizures, and the endless cups of tea or coffee which kept her going.

One of the bones of contention in reviewing Davoren's mass of work was his writing of poems about public events. Stephen Roche's triumphs, the Challenger space shuttle disaster, the Hillsborough tragedy, the Ethiopian famine, the Enniskillen bomb and the Birmingham Six injustice were all events which triggered the sidling or shooting (depending on his muscle tone) of his arm towards the poem-sign on his letter board. Invariably he would insist on us sending the poem off to some publication or individual. For example, we sent the Enniskillen poem off to the late Gordon Wilson (and received a very kind acknowledgement) while the Hillsborough poem was included in a volume of writings published to raise funds for the victims' families. Then there were the personal addresses, sometimes embarrassingly fulsome (even if they had distinctive Davoren touches), other times searingly insightful.

I was a bit precious about this public aspect of his writing, having a rather fastidious disdain for the role of the poet as social commentator. I also took a somewhat puritanical view of the promiscuity of his emotional and poetic outpourings. In the end Davoren faced me down with cheeky insouciance and I had to acknowledge that the fruits of his public concerns often got to the core in a way which bypassed the flood of journalism and TV coverage. As he said himself very early on: "Orzinary communicashyon is a slow way to zucsinctly indeecat my meening." So stalling and protesting a bit, I acted as his secretary and agent.

An unusual domestic incident that was honoured with a poem took place on one of our infrequent excursions to Donegal with Davoren. The episode occurred a few years prior to the preparation of the book but it has its place in this phase of our story. Tom was a very curious and greedy retired working donkey who hung around the cottage, butting his head against the door in the morning, looking for company and biscuits. He had also mastered the knack of opening the latch and doing his own exploring if we went out without bolting the door. Cornflake boxes covered in donkey slobber were not a pretty sight to find on returning to the house.

One sunny day around noon we put Davoren astride Tom and I walked alongside holding him as the donkey trod over the rough ground. It was all very convivial and Tom was rewarded with some biscuits. A short time later we were chopping vegetables when Tom nudged his way in the door. We were giving him a few scraps when Brighid had the bright idea of putting a piece of carrot in Dav's folded fist. Unfortunately Tom didn't distinguish between hand and carrot and as a result bit Davoren's hand, leaving teeth marks and drawing blood. Davoren was distraught, weeping copiously. I lifted him up over my shoulder and walked him back and forth outside the house while he shrieked his head off. Eventually I calmed him and we sat down on the rock which overlooked the Gweebarra estuary. I sat with my arm across Dav's chest. Tom approached us and, putting his head over my shoulder, nuzzled in towards Davoren. Companionable as he was, Tom had never engaged in such affection before; head-butting was more his style. It really did seem like a plea for forgiveness. Later the red-eyed Davoren again sat astride Tom on his rambles. His poem, 'Riding Rader (sic) Rascally Donkeys,' went as follows:

> *Dracula was practically an angel*
> *compared with dreadful Tom;*
> *he warranted my disapproval*
> *and lasting withdrawal from*
> *donkey-riding pleasures.*
> *When poignant tears were shed,*
> *limpid eyes implored forgiveness*
> *and I plucked up courage*
> *to master all my fears.*

□□□□

Davoren had the distinction of having some of his poems translated into German and published at a very early stage through the espousal of his talent by a remarkable German teacher, writer and actor resident in Ireland, Peter Jankowsky. Peter was born in Berlin during the war and with his wife, Veronica Bolay, came to Dublin in the early seventies. We met Veronica shortly before Davoren was born and an enduring bond was formed between Brighid and herself, occasioned by the fact that Veronica, who was also expecting her son Aengus at that time, didn't know any other Irish woman at a similar threshold.

Veronica turned to full-time painting a few years before the birth of Aengus, steadily building a reputation for her unusual angle of vision on, and colouring of, Irish landscapes and themes. Peter devoted himself to teaching German at the Goethe Institute and interpreting German culture to the Irish and Irish culture to the Germans. He had a leading role in the TV series on German spies in Ireland during the Second World War, *Caught in a Free State* by Brian Lynch, and is a regular radio contributor.

Peter was captivated by Davoren's distinctive 'voice' from the start. To this day I swear that Peter knows by heart more of Davoren's casual sayings, poems and cryptic remarks than I do, even though his meetings with Dav were not that frequent. Very early on Peter tried his hand at translating some of the poems into German. I would meet him and phrases from Davoren's poems such as "love glimmered on my tongue" or "a sunless shrieking sky" would be echoing around in his mind as he tried to find the best German equivalents. A few of Peter's translations appeared in a special edition of a German literary magazine, *Die Horen*, devoted to Ireland. After *Not Common Speech* was published, Peter translated the whole book, including the complicated introduction, and it was published by *Die Horen*. Peter also did some reading of Davoren's poetry on German radio.

An expedition we undertook several times with Davoren and Aengus was bird-watching on Sunday mornings on Bull Island. In truth Davoren couldn't see very much with his focusing problems but Peter was an expert on the species wintering on the island and Davoren learned a lot just listening to the chat as we wheeled him over the marshy terrain. Davoren wrote a little poem called 'Bird-watcher' for Aengus after one of these outings: "He freezes;/ cormorant, crow, chough/ are his nesting companions./ He looks." The word 'freezes' is apt because Davoren was generally petrified with the cold despite being well wrapped up.

Moreover, his lack of movement made him very vulnerable to getting chilled. But he threw himself into the adventure with zest and even more so one day when we got into a chase on the beach. As Peter was a little older, and I was a regular runner, I thought I could take him on in a sprint while pushing the wheelchair. As Aengus looked askance, these two 'crumbly' fathers made fools of themselves with Davoren a silent conscript. I was holding my own until suddenly the chair ran into a patch of soft sand. The front wheels dug in and jammed, the chair overturned and Davoren was pitched out nose first into the wet sand. Fortunately he came to no harm and found the whole episode hilarious. It was after one of these bird-watching episodes that Dav wrote 'Lines in Times of Great Happiness', a poem which I have always found powerfully expressive of his passion to soar and celebrate.

□□□□

The move to make a documentary about Davoren's life and writings stemmed directly from his appearance on 'Kenny Live'. The series producer interested in making the film, Kevin Linehan, had a sensitive grasp of what was involved for all concerned and so we gave our consent. We already had some experience of the amount of time it could take for a one- or two-minute news slot, nevertheless we weren't quite prepared for the amount of disruption the filming caused. The one small room in which all the Davoren-activity took place became an obstacle-course of lights, technicians, cables and cameramen. Kevin and his crew were painstaking in accommodating to Davoren's tempo and got some wonderful shots of him fired up with his zeal to communicate or making his 'little sound' of satisfaction. Dav the showman was in his element, revelling in having a platform to have his say without censure.

For the most part we entered into the filming in a carefree spirit. We got to know the crew and they adapted to our bohemian ways. Brighid's eagerness to find a role in the film for all the helpers involved with Davoren was amusing, no time more so than when Martyn Mulhere, a musician with long flowing red hair, was being interviewed in the garden. The interview was not going well. Martyn, normally a relaxed talker, was freezing in front of the camera. Suddenly Brighid appeared behind Martyn holding up a placard: "Available for gigs — Phone or call." After that the interview flowed more naturally.

⌐⌐⌐⌐

By chance, we met Daniel Day-Lewis, who later became the narrator for the documentary, at a function to commemorate Christy Brown in the Sandymount Clinic in 1989. Daniel was just beginning his intensive preparation for his part in *My Left Foot*, getting to know the character of Christy, and he had met and was thoroughly at ease with all of his brothers and sisters. He was also spending time in the classroom of the Sandymount Clinic, attuning himself to the kinds of disability which affected Christy.

Davoren, Brighid and he got into chat and for once it was Brighid who played the imp. While Davoren questioned Daniel earnestly about his father, the poet Cecil Day-Lewis, Brighid teased him on his risqué role in *The Unbearable Lightness of Being*. Daniel himself was thoroughly at home conducting this conversation with a fourteen-year-old Davoren twisting and straining on his mother's knee in the middle of a flurry of other people. In a letter which he wrote to Davoren after Brighid's death, he gave us a phrase — "scoopfuls of love" — which summed up something fundamental about Davoren's world.

⌐⌐⌐⌐

Davoren's fifteenth birthday on 12th March 1990 was a particularly happy affair. His friends Paul Coffey (fourteen on the 11th) and Mary Munnelly (thirteen on the 13th) were there. His book would be published in two weeks time. Máire Ní Bhraonáin of Clannad and a friend called in for the occasion. She had met Davoren after a Birmingham Six campaign concert and in one of those mysterious bondings, had fallen into cahoots

125

with him from the start. The evening of song and repartee, with Martyn Mulhere playing on the guitar, was just winding to a close when I came home from work.

The week of Davoren's book launch was an exciting week in Irish life with the winning of three Oscars by *My Left Foot* unleashing a spirit of national celebration almost on a par with the World Cup jamborees. The coincidence heightened the sense of Davoren as following in a line of disabled Irish writers.

Even though I can hardly be counted as an objective witness, I consider that for sheer festivity and variety, the launch of *Not Common Speech* on Wednesday, 27th March, 1990 was one of the best such events I ever attended. We had decided to make the book launch a 'family' and friends occasion rather than a media event. Davoren, looking elegant in his waistcoat and bow-tie, was the centre of the proceedings. During the formal part of the evening, he was imprisoned in his wheelchair, so that he looked strained and overcome, but a symphony of voices and sounds floated around him to set his heart dancing. His pals were present in numbers, Siobhán Walsh and Mary Munnelly among them.

Dermot Bolger spoke of how he had met Brighid and Davoren and had become committed to seeing his 'voice' in print. Brendan Kennelly gave his passionate responses to Davoren's appalling handicap (no sentimentality) and soaring poetry (no holding back), and read several poems. I still remember vividly the chill down my spine as he gave 'Sapling Bent by a Cruel Wind' his full measure. Ivor Browne played the tin whistle, Máire Ní Bhraonáin and the Voice Squad sang. Barry Gleeson also read a few poems in his strong deep tones and spoke about Davoren's arresting presence in the classroom. I read a few poems that were not included in the book that I thought might appeal to the younger friends. The best reaction was to a ballad-type poem he had written about my succession of battered cars, including one in which the radiator had exploded in Donegal at 11.30 at night half-way up a mountain with Davoren and a helper, Denise Brady, contributing a mixture of panic and hilarity. (Unfortunately, the only copy of it got mislaid that evening.) Brighid rounded off the evening thanking all who had helped Davoren. I thought she looked happy but strained — puffy and flushed — but wasn't surprised.

The more lively part of the evening for Davoren came later when he regained his springboard — the laps of heart-bonding and heart-outpouring. That night he was able to sign copies of the book with a stamp that we had got made to his specifications:

My heart goes with this gift of my words

Davoren Hanna

Bereft by Gweebarra

There was a powerful undertow of stress and turbulence for Brighid in the wake of the publication of Davoren's book and the attendant interviews and public appearances. She took great delight in his sense of triumph and his enjoyment of his celebrity status, having staked huge reserves of her energy in order to create a platform from which his talents could be fostered, yet hoping that in time she could pass on the baton of Davoren's communication to technology. She knew that she needed a rest from the endless striving, pushing, cajoling and campaigning that she had been doing for Davoren. But in her heart she knew that the screws were tightening. Davoren's efforts to 'master' the switches and computer technology were not going well and her own energies for working with him were under increasing strain. The recuperation periods she needed between sessions with Davoren were becoming longer; the strain on her back, arms and metabolism was severe. She was spending a lot of money on getting back-up at home, especially in the evenings when I was working, but was not greatly benefitting from this as she continually stepped in both to inspire the young people working with Davoren, and to keep his flow of communication going.

We had a lot of rows over the time she spent on the phone which came back to haunt me in disturbing ways after her death. There was a mean-spirited side to my protests as I felt that the 'Davoren project' was like a juggernaut crushing our personal lives and privacy. But my intentions were at least partly honourable as I saw clearly that she was wearing herself down. She was restless and driven but also partly demented. She was never businesslike on the phone, she listened to the stories of her interlocutors and she told her own stories colourfully and at length. For all that she was garnering immense support for Davoren, she was depleting precious resources.

My bickering with her over the lengthy phone calls rebuked me later in the way in which all such petty wrangles do, but the way in which it came back at me was cunningly ironic. After her death, I became the organiser of schedules of care and the manager of finances for Davoren, and so I was involved in complicated rounds of phone calls. But even more pointedly I, who had previously been sparing and to-the-point, now poured out my heart to our friends and supporters on the phone. The phone became one of the refuges to which I fled in order to break the isolation and desolation which I felt so keenly despite the back-up in the household.

The cottage in Mulnamina More was Brighid's great retreat, away from phone calls and stress. During the autumn and spring, she occasionally went up on her own while I minded the fort at home. She had overcome her fear of spending the night alone in the isolated cottage and invariably came back to Davoren and me renewed for the fray.

Each summer was like a black hole for Brighid with Davoren off school for three months with no weekly routine. We holidayed and went on trips with Davoren and she organised expeditions for him with usually two helpers accompanying him. But we also needed time together on our own to recuperate. In 1990 we were lucky. We were able to take a few days in early June and then a week straddling the end of June and early July while Davoren spent a fortnight at an Irish college in the Kerry Gaeltacht.

My recollection of the visit in early June is not that clear except that there was considerable tension between us. Brighid had acquired the cottage from her brother-in-law because she loved Donegal so much and she hated to see the house going into foreign hands. I had argued against our involvement because the cottage was so dilapidated, so far away, difficult of access for Davoren and an extra burden on us. But I knew it was useless arguing when Brighid's heart was set on something, so I had backed her up in the end.

I vied with Brighid in my passion for Donegal, but it was roaming the wide open spaces, climbing the wooded hills near the cottage, and swimming on the beaches, and in the lakes and streams that I loved. More even than in our Dublin home, Brighid created a stage-set of charm and homeliness in the cottage. But all the while the structural flaws in both our houses were piling up. My joke about our small house in Drumcondra was that the living-room was the stage set and all the other rooms were piled high with props — a lot of Davoren's equipment, books, photographs, Davoren's and my writings and Brighid's study and work-notes.

Brighid berated herself for the chaos of our Dublin home but could not find the mental space to do anything about it. Her most consoling story about it concerned a chat she had with the serene but lively elderly widow who lived beside us, Nellie Shelley. Brighid was upset at not being able to keep the house in order and Mrs Shelley told her not to worry, for she herself had stood in front of her dusty dressing-table mirror that morning and written with her finger on the dust: "Shame on you, Nellie!"

As my handyman interest is desultory and my skill limited, I did not relish going up to Donegal to do repair work. Brighid had done measurements and friends had made replacements for the windows which were currently held together with stones and bits of stick. But she had made an error in her measurements and I now had the job of fitting windows that didn't fit. I did major renovations so infrequently that every time I undertook a job, I had to relearn all the skills.

One afternoon the work was not going well, as I tried to fill the gaps with stones to prevent the crumbling cottage plaster from collapsing on top of me before finishing off the job with freshly-made concrete. We needed to go shopping in Dungloe and, since Brighid had given up on her attempt to learn to drive, I had to break off from my work to go on the expedition. We went to Dooey beach en route in the hope of finding solace there. I tried to disentangle a kite which I had bought a few months previously for Davoren in the hope that he might be able to hold it and have some simulacrum of control.

The kite had been a disaster. It was a ridiculous last emblem of my physical hopes for Davoren — the dream of doing normal father-and-son things without this terrible communication barrier. As I persisted in trying to free the kite on the cold windswept beach, all the ravages and disappointments of my life seemed to well up in me and when Brighid tried to persuade me to desist from my disentangling, I screamed and howled into the wind. No doubt this was a sad and bitter occasion but I still believe that if you are racked by grief, an isolated beach is a good place to vent that shrieking self.

I often thought afterwards that I was granted a special grace that Brighid did not die on that visit to Donegal. I know that I would have been able to rediscover a balance in recollecting the deep passionate connection we had, and our support of one another through mostly tough times, but it would have been an extra pain on me.

Putting that tormenting wrangle on the beach behind us, we returned to mounting World Cup fever in Dublin, before going to Cork (my native city) for a reading in a bookshop. We brought along Martyn Mulhere, the talented young musician whom Brighid had taken under her wing and who was going to work with Davoren in school the following year. Martyn played classical music while people mingled before the reading, where we were very warmly received. We also did a radio interview and the Davoren-Brighid combination seemed as powerful and magnetic as ever.

The weekend of Ireland's quarter-final match with Italy in Rome, Brighid attended a large international women's conference at Termonfeckin while Davoren and I joined in the football hooley in Dublin. I remember the coincidence well because there was apparently a big debate at the conference about whether it was politically correct to have the attendance gathered around the TV watching the football.

One of the main organisers of the conference, feminist theologian Mary Condren, was a good friend of Brighid's and in the midst of other responsibilities kept a watchful eye on her. Mary could see that, behind the public face of Brighid, which was exuberant about Davoren's triumph and fertile with ideas about her own sphere of work, the knell of exhaustion was tolling inexorably. Death always casts a retrospective glow on events, but I have no doubt from reports and from the evidence of my own eyes that during that spring and summer, Brighid was at the height of her creative powers. She impressed participants at the conference with her inventiveness in dealing with sexuality education, with her humour and lightness of touch. It was liberating for her to throw aside the martyr-mother role in which, despite her own intentions, she found herself cast when campaigning for Davoren. But Mary Condren could also see what was all too clear to me at home — that the sparkling, playful Brighid was only surfacing intermittently.

One afternoon Brighid could not take any more earnest discussions and she persuaded Mary against her better judgement to join her on a skite into Drogheda. Brighid needed her cups of tea and coffee, her rest and relaxation. On the way back a sudden shout from Brighid forced Mary to stop the car, whereupon Brighid dashed out to collect a sprightly cluster of red poppies by the roadside — a strong talisman for her journey.

In the meantime Davoren was also in high spirits. One night a young friend, Eoin, brought Davoren to a pub where some friends were playing a gig. They were very welcoming to Davoren and towards the end of evening the lead singer read his World Cup poem, 'Jack's Boys,' which concludes with a dig at Brighid's feigned aloofness to the passions aroused by bunches of men chasing after an inflated bit of leather.:

> *Mythic goals — very nearly scored,*
> *desperately saved or futilely wasted—*
> *are furiously discussed.*
> *Arguments glide over iced hearts*
> *indifferent to hearts aglow*
> *with the fire of hopeful victory.*
> *Somewhere, a whistle blows—*
> *WE'VE WON !!!*

With that, the bar erupted with "Ole, ole, ole — We're all part of Jackie's Army." The acclaim went on for nearly five minutes. Never before (nor since) have I heard a poem received with such rapture.

□□□□

Davoren was heading for Ventry in the Dingle peninsula after that weekend for his break in the Gaeltacht. Clíona Saidléar and Helena Boyd were accompanying him so we were confident he would be well cared for *and* have a lively time. We decided not to rush things by trying to set off for Donegal on the same day that we saw Davoren off on his travels (always a heavy logistical operation with his equipment); thus we departed Tuesday morning refreshed and for the first time in years, we conversed a lot on the journey.

Brighid talked about new work projects — she wanted to make educational films or videos, get more involved in teacher-education. We had an engaging debate about art which started from my surprise at her bringing along *The Best of Myles* as holiday reading. Brighid had introduced me to Flann O'Brien in our early days and I was enchanted for a while, but latterly I had decided there was something curmudgeonly about the man, which came through in his writing. We both agreed something vague in the end: that art involves some imaginative transformation of the real. As it turned out, during the holiday we both read Myles, laughed a lot and were transformed.

The week was a calm and peaceful one. There was no urgent repair work to be done so I was free of anxiety. There was a cold wind blowing most of the week so we didn't go on any major trips nor to the beach together as Brighid only liked to go on real 'Dooey days'. I went for the swims and runs regardless, usually taking in the beach on my shopping expeditions. Brighid rested a lot, letting the atmosphere of the estuary and the cottage sink in and gradually making small transformations, a little curtain here and a gnarled piece of wood placed somewhere else. While we visited Brighid's sister and her children in Letterkenny, there was plenty of time for reading and chatting around the fireside, and the stress seemed to be easing out of Brighid. We rang Davoren's helpers in Kerry and though the bad weather was spoiling things down there as well, we were happy that Davoren was in good hands and in good spirits.

Gweebarra was a haven for Brighid but she also used it to try to catch up on neglected tasks, whether educational work or a batch of Davoren's or personal correspondence. My recollection is that on this trip, despite the swirling intensity of Davoren's activities during the previous few months, Brighid didn't come charged with a heavy burden of work. *Reculer pour mieux sauter*, a favourite phrase of mine, had been an anthem between us on the car journey up to Donegal. We both knew that we needed to recuperate from the constancy of Davoren's needs. Brighid carried her mighty and stressful campaign on behalf of Davoren to

Donegal, but on it too descended some of Mulnamina's peace, so well evoked in his poem of the same name:

> *Lazy silver clouds mass over the estuary*
> *sending curlews querulously ashore*
> *towards evening sanctuary;*
> *warmth, especially turf fire generated,*
> *shall linger in my memory*
> *as an instance of Mulnamina's charm.*

Sunday, 8th July, continued the pattern. Brighid decided she was going to paint the front door of the cottage in a strong Royal Mail Red. I set off on my usual shop-and-sea expedition. It was a bright sunny day but there was a biting north-west wind whipping in from the Atlantic so that even I thought it folly to take a dip. Nevertheless the attraction of the breakers overcame good sense and I had a bracing swim and returned to the cottage in buoyant form. Brighid had finished painting the door but had found it tiring, complaining of a strain in her neck, shoulder and chest. But she really had become very unfit and I didn't think much of it. Despite the pain, she was very proud of her finished work: the bright red door.

I cooked lunch and afterwards Brighid felt her stomach somewhat upset, but we settled into fireside chat and musing. I tried to ease the pain in her neck and shoulders with some gentle massage while Brighid moved into a rhythmic recapitulation of her life. She regretted some of the barren years spent preparing her M.Ed. thesis. Vivid, face-to-face communication and not academic writing was her forte. She sang of motherhood and its gut-wrenching joys and pain. Our young lovers' dreams were also part of the litany. Her recurring mantra — "I should have been a nun, I should have been a nun" — had us both laughing. This refrain was her plea for space and for release from stress to allow her meditative self to flourish, yet I teased her by suggesting that she would surely have been a rebel in the cloister.

Gradually the flow of words ebbed and we lay down. Without any gilding of the lily, I can honestly say that we were as happy and as close as we had ever been. I, in particular, felt a deep peace ease away the ache in my heart for more children.

Brighid wasn't feeling too well but needed to take her insulin injection and then eat afterwards, so I prepared another light meal. Brighid couldn't hold down her food but was later able to take some milk. Failure to absorb food after taking insulin is itself a critical matter as it can lead to a coma but the crisis seemed to have passed. Plans to go out for the evening to watch the World Cup Final in a pub or to attend a fund-raising dance for a local handicapped child were abandoned, but I decided I would drop down to Annie and Danny's for the second-half of the match. Annie and Danny O'Donnell were the parents of Brighid's brother-in-law. Brighid had adopted them as proxy parents and they her; their cottage was a hospitable hearth of continuous stories and tea-drinking. Brighid suggested that I ask them if they had some porridge, in case she needed to have some easily digestible food later on.

After the hours of closeness with Brighid, seeing out the World Cup had dropped down on my list of priorities so I again asked Brighid if it was all right to go out. She assured me that she'd be fine so I went down the hill to Annie and Danny's with a song in my heart.

David Robertson, our immediate neighbour on Mulnamina, came down about three-quarters-of-an-hour later to tell me that Brighid had come into their cottage (about 150 yards from ours) in a very sick and disorientated condition. She had been unable to hold down the food and had begun to slip into a daze. Yet she had sufficient presence of mind to go for help and was able to explain her predicament. A dentist-friend staying with David understood the danger immediately and tried to get her to take sugar lumps and in fact she seemed to have improved before David came down for me. Nonetheless he knew she needed medical care urgently.

I ran up the hill with David and I could see immediately that the situation was serious. Brighid's speech was slurred and her eyes fuzzy. The first priority was to get her down the hill to a more accessible house to call an ambulance or doctor, so David brought his car to the door of his cottage. The extraordinary detail I remember most clearly was Brighid mumbling to me to bring a towel; at that last moment she was concerned lest she soil David's car. As we bundled her into the car, Brighid collapsed and her body became a dead weight. I think I knew in my heart that she was gone but I clung on to her — and to hope — as we made our bumpy way down the hill.

Somehow we got her out of the car and laid her down on the floor of Annie and Danny's. We tried all we could to revive her as we awaited the arrival of the doctor, Dr Kevin Boner, from across the other side of the estuary. I still could not believe it when the doctor confirmed that she was dead and I shrieked continuously, "No, no, no, it can't be true!" He said she had died very quickly of a massive heart attack. Her great heart had given out.

Dr Boner could see my devastation with his own eyes and Annie and Danny briefly filled him in about Davoren. He was a very consoling, compassionate presence, as we all prayed together on the floor around Brighid's body, which was already beginning to have the chill and pallor of death.

Moments of ferocious clarity alternated with swirling confusion and horror as I tried to cope. We decided there was no point in telephoning Davoren, Clíona and Helena in Kerry; they would only have to get through an extra night of utter bafflement. As I telephoned Brighid's brother in Australia and my own brother Paul in Dublin, Brighid's body was taken away to the mortuary in Dungloe. Meanwhile the complications of making arrangements involving Donegal, Dublin and Kerry were considerable.

I made the decision that I needed (and was strong enough) to spend the night in the cottage on my own. As I climbed up the steep path overlooking the Gweebarra estuary, I made a promise to Brighid and to Davoren that I would not be defeated by this challenge that Brighid had passed on to me. I knew that the quiet, behind-the-scenes supportive role that I had played in relation to Brighid's mighty endeavour for Davoren was gone for ever. Somehow I saw more clearly than at any previous stage of my life that helplessness, passivity and feeling sorry for myself would not save me now. For Davoren and for my own sake, I resolved to cheerfully battle on. During black periods over the next four years, those moments of clarity on the climb over Gweebarra were often my only refuge.

One of the few things I recollect clearly from that night was glancing at the Sunday newspapers strewn around the cottage: full of rumours that Brian Keenan was about to be freed. I kept saying to myself — I hope something good happens in this world, let something good happen — and I turned on the radio in the morning hoping that his release would be announced.

Around five or six in the morning (it was already fully bright) I began to break down, wandering around talking to myself, physically crumbling and breaking into tears but overall the night had strengthened me for the days ahead, for dealing with Davoren on his return from Kerry. Around 7.30 in warm morning sunshine I crossed the Gweebarra to telephone Davoren's godfather, Joe Dunne, from a public kiosk. The weather had suddenly been transformed: Donegal was all warmth and sunshine but there were to be no more 'Dooey days' for Brighid.

Talking to Davoren and his helpers in Kerry was the next big hurdle. I have no recollection of what I said on the phone to Clíona. She and Helena reported to me that Davoren withdrew into almost total blankness when he was told. All three of them were in terrible shock. They hugged, chatted and consoled each other as best they could throughout the day. We eventually discovered that we could not get transport to Dublin for them that day so they had to endure hours of bleakness on the Monday evening and night and then travel on the train the next day, with people staring at them as they read in the papers of Brighid's death. Meanwhile my brothers, Peter and Paul, and my friends, Joe Dunne and John Doyle, came to Mulnamina to accompany and support me on the journey home.

When Davoren arrived back in Dublin early on the Tuesday evening, we had a special ceremony in the church with the coffin open; Davoren was still, numb and thoughtful as he somehow accepted that his greatest champion, the inspirational mother who had cradled him into life and even more literally into communication, was no more.

With the help of Fr Dara Molloy from the Aran Islands, Mary Condren and many other friends, we had very beautiful and consoling ceremonies. Fr Brian Power, the UCD chaplain who had married us in University Church, Stephen's Green, twenty years previously, spoke very simply of a last chance-meeting with Brighid as she hurried for the bus to Donegal a few months previously. Brighid had no truck with a patriarchal priesthood so her belief in the power of women to voice the spirit was well represented by Mary and her good friend Margaret Armstrong. Some of Davoren's poems about his mother were read and Fionn O'Leary sang a Bach aria.

At the crematorium, I particularly liked a ceremony of Dara's involving bowls of oil and water. The water symbolised forgiveness and reconciliation — for any wrong we felt we had ever done to Brighid, or for something that we had failed to do. The oil symbolised healing for our own pain, loss and sorrow. My father, who was already quite frail, was one of the first to hop out of his seat to take part in this innovative ceremonial. He and Brighid, two of the strongest characters you would ever be likely to meet, had often locked horns but in the end had reached a state of grudging respect. These gestures of seeking forgiveness and healing had of course deep, deep resonances for Davoren and myself in our different ways and would stay with us as comforting signposts to look back on.

Davoren's communication-allies, Sorcha Saidléar, Gary Rutherford and Anna Brady, were around a lot and he had many chats with them, for some of which I would not have been present. Records of most of these conversations were either not kept or have since been mislaid. Yet one chat etched itself deeply into the mind of Eoin O'Byrne, a young helper whom I mentioned previously. Eoin's own mother had died in tragic circumstances a few years earlier when he was fifteen, Davoren's age at the time of Brighid's death.

Eoin had, in his own words, "tons of idealism and masses of immaturity', but on that day he shared with Davoren some of the guilt which he had experienced after his mother's death over the hassles he had caused her. This conversation took place with Sorcha Saidléar acting as intermediary and I only heard about it over a year after Davoren's own death. Eoin told Davoren that after his mother's death, he thought the world had ended and that he would never smile again. Davoren responded: "My heart is eaten up with sadness but you've given me hope" and later "Feck it, I must get on with life."

□□□□

At the funeral, Mary Condren had placed a sheaf of fabric poppies on Brighid's coffin in memory of Brighid's last mad dash to collect the wild poppies by the roadside but also, in line with the myth of Demeter and Persephone, as food for Brighid's journey. With Gary, Davoren wrote the poem 'Poppy Girl'. Although Brighid's body had been cremated, Davoren imagined us at the traditional graveside. The strong red of the poppy had always had an attraction for Brighid; in addition she liked their wild, wayside nature.

> *Sad faces, all gathered —*
> *left as mourners by the graveside —*
> *bid adieu as a poppy girl departs.*
> *Her sapling, bent by a cruel wind,*
> *now clinging slavishly to a father's pain,*
> *waits for a God missing to show his love.*
> *Assassinated motherhood, assimilated mourning,*
> *lasting remains etched in our minds;*
> *regret washed in water;*
> *pain soothed in healing oil.*
> *Love of a poppy girl lies now in ashes,*
> *awaiting the Saviour*
> *sailing soul-winds over the cliffs of Gaoth-barra.*

A month after Brighid's death, we brought her ashes up to Donegal and scattered them around the Mulnamina rock where she used to sit, enjoying the constantly mobile vista of the estuary as the sandbanks were covered and uncovered by the tide and the waters were still or whipped up depending on the wind. I sang, we read Davoren's Mulnamina poem, Margaret Armstrong played 'Where'er You Walk' by Handel on the recorder and we shared reminiscences. We then walked down to the pier and scattered the last of the ashes on the outgoing tide in the Gweebarra estuary. The traditional song that Máire Ní Bhraonáin had so prophetically sung at Davoren's book launch, 'Gaoith Barra na dTonn,' is a fitting commentary on that final ceremony with Brighid's remains. Máire's free translation of the last verse is that the singer prefers at the end of her days for her soul to be carried on a leaf by the wooded shores of the Gweebarra rather than to attain the blessedness of heaven itself:

> 'S guímse Pádraig agus Naomh Chonaill caol
> Nach n-iarraim aon Fhlaitheas i ndeireadh mo shaoil
> Ach m' anam bheith seoladh fá'n duilliúr donn
> Tá ag fás fá do chladaí, a Ghaoth Barra na dTonn.

I later wrote a little booklet describing the music, song, poetry and stillness of that evening. It was a very simple gathering with just Margaret Armstrong, our good friends Cian Cafferky and Annette Healy, and Davoren and myself present, but somehow it seemed to mark a turning-point for Davoren. The rhythm of 'getting on with life' after a sudden death is an elusive matter at the best of times. After four-and-a-half years in which I lost my wife, my mother, my only son and my father, I have considerable experience of its waxing and waning. The way in which Davoren and I found new surges of energy in the year immediately after Brighid's death was uncanny and at times unsettling.

Until early in the following summer, Davoren's health was as strong as it had ever been, while I myself experienced rushes of adrenalin and discovered capacities to organise and co-ordinate all the strands of Davoren's and my own life which I would not have imagined possible. I was occasionally overcome, as was Davoren, by sudden and inconsolable grief and devastating exhaustion but the full debilitating attrition wrought by our loss only seeped into our lives about a year afterwards. At times we spoke of Brighid's spirit or strength still guiding us; mostly we just accepted the strangeness of life going on.

Shooting Star

Davoren's 'getting on with life' was given a sharp edge by a chain of events spanning most of 1990: the publication of his book in the springtime, the publicity about Brighid's death and the broadcast of the RTÉ documentary on his story, 'Poised for Flight' in September. We saw the programme with the producer, Kevin Linehan, out in Donnybrook a few days before it was broadcast. The final editing of the film and adding of the script read by Daniel Day-Lewis had been completed just a week before Brighid died so it was a terrible shock to hear the last words spoken by Brighid to camera:

> My resolve is to try and see, without killing myself, to what extent I can help this (his vision) to be realised. I know that's what he would want and I'd die happy if I thought it was possible.

Neither Davoren nor I had been present when the interview with Brighid was recorded so we had no idea what she had said. Kevin had warned me that her testimony about her life-and-death struggle had been chosen as the ending for the documentary prior to her death and in the hasty way in which you make these decisions, I had accepted it as a *fait accompli* but, seeing it broadcast, I experienced it as a turning of the knife into whatever guilt Davoren might have felt about the strain which he had unwittingly imposed on his mother.

The final happy moments which were filmed in the Phoenix Park had nothing of the staged-for-camera family outing atmosphere which can happen in these documentaries. It was a genuinely carefree, madcap afternoon with Davoren, his friend Mary Munnelly, Brighid, Cian, Annette and myself. We ended up sitting on the grass in front of Kavanagh's pub in Glasnevin, otherwise known as the Gravediggers, drinking Guinness and giggling with Mary. Somehow the memory of the genuine radiance of that afternoon assuaged the bitterness of witnessing Brighid's plea for help.

The other depressing aspect of viewing the documentary was that the time-frame used by Kevin Linehan for the different sections of the film was the quest for a technological breakthrough in Davoren's communication. The documentary showed the different forms of head and eye movement which had been explored by David Vernon. The film ended on an ambiguous note, with the crew having captured Davoren on one of his good days, but I had reason to believe that Davoren's faith in "inventive saviours" was waning.

Another cruel twist in the light of Davoren's new burdens was Gary's final remark: "To see a guy like that who gets so many knocks and kicks and scratches and bruises in life and he still has a zest and a taste for life and he wants more. He's only had the starting course. Now he wants the main meal."

Overall, however, we were very happy with the documentary. The power of Davoren's poetry was put across by Brendan Kennelly's passionate readings, the impishness of his personality was well communicated in several shots of conversations with Brighid and other helpers, and the mixture of anger and anguish we experienced when Davoren's 'voice' was treated with suspicion was given a good airing.

In the wake of this flurry of publicity, an old conflict that had plagued relations between me and Brighid and Davoren resurfaced. Despite, or maybe because of, my own involvement in journalism, I tended towards caution, reticence and perhaps even fear in courting publicity on the media. Brighid often accused me of wanting to hide my light under a bushel. I in turn countered that she was a 'notice-box' and that Davoren had inherited to the full this aspect of her personality.

Mostly it was just rough-and-tumble banter but there lurked an underlying edge. I knew that Brighid had harboured deep reservations about the publicity because of the strain on her personally but she felt that she had no alternative, both for the sake of Davoren's and her own credibility and for financial reasons. To the end she clung to the hope that there was someone out there who would discover the key to Davoren's communication difficulties. She also had a passion and pain in her heart in the face of the communication difficulties of kindred spirits of Davoren. She dreamed of generations of Davorens (though maybe not great poetic spirits) who never got the chance to express themselves. She used to exasperate June Levine, who had done a spectacular job fund-raising for Davoren, by unearthing new cases of need and silent imprisonment. In a way I recognised that Brighid's public appearances for Davoren were a continuation of her prayers, non-prayers and curses of the night, when she berated God for creating such a charade. Brighid's advocacy of Davoren combined the mystical and the practical, the dove and serpent; it was a plea for help to the heavens and to the world.

In any case I was determined that Davoren and myself, especially after Brighid's death, would not became a freak-show of tragedy and poignancy. In part this resolve sprang from my old reticence and a sense of self-preservation in respect of my privacy and dignity. But the better part of it was fuelled by those flashes of clarity on my climb up Mulnamina More on the night of Brighid's death: to cheerfully take up the baton to run the race in the best way that *I* could was "my star-signpost to hope".

This conflict over public recognition came to a head one afternoon when Davoren and I were shopping on Grafton Street in autumn 1990. If it is possible to imagine it, my attitude on this street of style and poses was one of skulking, until suddenly we met some casual friends from the old days in UCD. They were people I hadn't seen for almost twenty years but they were delighted to meet the celebrity-poet Davoren Hanna. Up to this point, Davoren had himself been scowling impassively at the Saturday afternoon strollers. Now he deployed his full palette of charm and radiance. Chatting to him afterwards, I said we'd have to accept that we were irreconcilably different but that in so far as it was necessary, I'd bat for him in the public limelight.

That autumn the high-profile events included a poetry reading in Bewley's on Mary Street organised by Poetry Ireland. An overflow audience came along to the evening which was a tribute to Brighid and a fund-raiser. Then in November Davoren was named 'Dubliner of the Month' on 98FM radio station and in the same month he was among the recipients of a People of the Year award sponsored by the Rehabilitation Institute at the Burlington Hotel. The latter ceremony was a long ordeal as rehearsals and photo-calls took place prior to the live screening. While Davoren was very composed throughout the day, I was acutely nervous, afraid that Davoren would 'peak too soon,' that he would be exhausted by the time the actual presentation came around and that he would end up appearing contorted and miserable. In the event it was I who crumbled. Accompanying him onto the stage to receive his award, as I came to the end of Davoren's message, I faltered, and Thelma Mansfield had to finish it off for us:

> I am so honoured as the recipient of this award I find myself speechless! My life-loving parents, helpers and friends have pinnacled me onto this stage tonight. To fight, as they have for me, strengthens my resolve. I feel a strong sense that people have a faith in me which allows me to climb my Everests, which I must face. In order to convey my gratitude and sincere thanks to everyone, I would open my heart-tavern and toast your health. Finally, I wish to dedicate this award to my mother, Brighid, whose life was dedicated to me.

For his part Davoren went from strength to strength as the evening progressed. With his old school pal from St Pat's in Drumcondra, Paul Coffey, and friends and helpers, Clíona and Sorcha Saidléar, Davoren radiated all his old charm. Typing at his board with Sorcha he was ready with his cajolery and barbed comments. There was a renewal of banter and repartee with John B Keane, another person honoured that year. Sorcha attached a felt pen to Davoren's hand and he joined spiritedly in the signing of his 'autograph' on books and menu cards.

We were particularly delighted to meet Brian Keenan and his sisters, who were the recipients of the special award that year. I told Brian of my strange incantation during the night of Brighid's death and how Davoren and I had both rejoiced at his eventual release and taken heart from his testimony about the friendship and solidarity which had sustained him. At one in the morning as the hotel staff were moving in to tidy up, Davoren was still thrashing away on Sorcha's lap.

□□□□

That night of dynamic communication brought home to me how restricted Davoren's possibilities now were, given that I was almost completely deadlocked with him. Sorcha, Anna and Gary were now the only people who could work with him and all had now moved on to heavy new responsibilities in their own lives, even though they continued to make themselves available as much as possible. Martyn Mulhere, who worked with Davoren in school during the years 1990 to 1992, had been depending on Brighid to coach him into working at the board with Davoren. He had been in Greece playing music when Brighid died and he took a long time to regain his bearings on his return.

As such, Davoren's possibilities of participating in school doing normal school work or through making poetic or other pungent interventions in the cut-and-thrust with his classmates were being gradually snuffed out. While he continued to receive rock-solid support and encouragement that went far beyond the teaching role from the staff at Rosmini, particularly Barry Gleeson and Niamh Digan, he was more adrift from normal school life than he had been heretofore.

□□□□

Another bell tolling in our lives was the ebbing away of my mother's life. She had become crippled with arthritis, chronically stooped and also severely confused over a period of several years prior to Brighid's death and, with my father also ailing, but mentally very alert, it had been necessary to find nursing home care for her. In fact I was psychologically bracing myself for her demise during the months prior to Brighid's sudden death.

When we went out to Dalkey to see her the day after Brighid's funeral, she was happy to see us, took her usual simple delight in Davoren, but otherwise seemed numbed about what had happened. Brighid and herself had been utterly dissimilar characters (my mother was petite and retiring while Brighid was a larger-than-life performer) but in better days they had managed to knock a good deal of fun out of one another. Brighid had the capacity to unearth the girlish spirit in my mother which had become overladen with a sense of mothering and wifely duties. On that day in July, 1990, it wasn't clear to me whether my mother fully understood that Brighid had indeed died and over the next few months she often asked for her. She was generally miserable over the last year or so of her life and in a naïve way I consoled myself that she was better off not fully understanding.

In fact I was wrong, as I learned only several years later. When my mother was told of Brighid's death, she fully understood the tragedy that had happened to us and was so upset that she wanted to die. Already in considerable pain and distress (her knee-joints cracked horrendously as she got up or down from a chair), she had seen enough of life and its miseries, and she could not imagine how Davoren and I could continue on without Brighid. But the processes of senile degeneration were taking a toll: thus, while she had certainly taken in the fact that Brighid had passed away on that first day, afterwards she only understood in flashes; every so often she would conveniently forget. At the time of immediate crisis after Brighid's death when she was so spent and heart-broken, my sister-in-law Joan was despatched urgently to plead with her to hang on for a while. She had grit too, my mother, despite her unassuming exterior, and she promised that she would.

And she did hang on, only to die peacefully in her sleep just over five months after Brighid's death, on 19th January 1991. Because of Davoren's difficulties, our residence across the other side of the city and her increasing frailty, she had never had a strong 'granny' role, yet she had been a gentle, loving presence in his life. There was a quiet radiance between them; they seemed able to console and cheer each other up without words.

The night of her death I returned from the family home in Dalkey to Drumcondra about nine o'clock. The house was empty, Davoren was being minded elsewhere for a few hours, and I sat quietly taking it all in. Suddenly I was disturbed by a noise under the stairs. Our cat, Trixie, an important member of our household over many years, had abandoned us after Brighid's death, taking up residence with a neighbour, and we scarcely ever saw her any more. That evening, however, she had managed to get into the house and was making her presence felt. Somehow I found it consoling.

On the following day, I struggled laboriously at the typewriter with Davoren. "Great was God to have given the best to us," was all I could get out of him. He and I soldiered together through the funeral ceremonies for my mother over the next few days, facing the public gaze, trying to remain cheerful. Fortunately the day of the burial in Shanganagh cemetery was a bright, warm day, despite it being the middle of January. I felt huge solidarity stretching across the generations with Davoren and my father, two figures who scarcely understood each other at all, but with whom I was united in grief and somehow a will to go on.

Boon from Brittany

A new stream bubbled into our lives in the autumn of 1990. It started casually enough, but as it turned out, it remained with us as a revitalizing force for the rest of Davoren's life. I was scrambling and improvising frantically to keep the home intact and hold on to my job at the same time. Indeed, a particularly dramatic episode in the unhappy history of the *Irish Press* organization took place just a week after Brighid's death. On foot of a management threat to close the papers unless we accepted their latest half-baked rescue plan, we came within a few hours of that fate (which turned out of course to be only a deferred execution). Despite the extraordinarily painful days I was living through, I seemed to be very lucid and spoke out strongly at meetings in favour of basic trade union principles. All of the solidarity which Brighid and I had drummed into Davoren came to the fore at home as he supported me — his "leaden-hearted worker" — through the crisis. Maybe the fight for dignity and livelihood gave us something outside ourselves on which to focus.

Bewley's in Westmoreland Street was a frequent gathering-place for au pairs and one of my work colleagues had got to know a group of them from calling in there regularly before starting his evening shift. Jane Voisin, a twenty-one-year-old girl from Redon in the south-east corner of Brittany, needed a change of family and so it was arranged that I meet her. This suggestion was a new departure for though we had lived through many years with helpers and friends constantly around the house, we had never had someone living in. I had, however, a deep connection with France: Brighid had started off as a French teacher, we had spent a year living in Paris while I researched French philosophy and I had kept up a strong interest through my work in the International Telephone Exchange and through reading.

Interested in trying out this unusual au pair position, Jane came to the house where she took Davoren in her stride and thus began our Breton adventure. Jane had an air of being cool, detached and unflappable; she was cheeky towards me and irreverent about the mythology of Davoren. Behind that facade she was warm, loving and resourceful. She mixed in Bohemian circles in the city but was very conscientious and dependable. She came among us at a time when we were very broken and introduced a light touch of humour and mischief. Jostling good-humouredly for pre-eminence with the other helpers, she proved a pioneering spirit in a whole new expansion in Davoren's family. All of Davoren's male friends and helpers delighted in this new element in his circle, and while the girls pretended to feel threatened by the exotic newcomer, in reality they too enjoyed the new buzz in the house. Another pattern which began with Jane was that Davoren's au pair tended to become the *mère poule* or mother hen for other more homesick or disgruntled au pairs in the city.

Jane arranged for a friend from her village, Sylvie Marsac, to come for six weeks during the summer of 1991. Sylvie was fortunate to come at a time when I planned several trips and outings for Davoren to get us over the summer anniversary period. For Brighid's anniversary, Fr Brian Power said Mass in the house. Friends and family spilled out of the one small room in which all the love and craziness of the house took place. As Margaret Armstrong played the recorder in the hallway, Brian thoughtfully recalled Brighid's life and brought everyone together to pray as best they could. Kneeling beside Davoren, I wept throughout the entire Mass (something I had not done at the funeral ceremonies); it was partly gratitude for our survival with somehow our hearts intact, and partly grief at last seeping out.

Sylvie Marsac's stay was short, her English not as strong as Jane's, but her heart was warm and she was intuitively sensitive to the atmosphere of sadness interspersed with episodes of wild hilarity which kept us going. Davoren nestled into her warm embrace at this desolate time for him. This period also saw the beginning of two new trials for Davoren, searing pains in his legs and an ulcer in his stomach. He needed more than ever all the comfort he could find.

Sylvie One, as we came to call her in our private history of the Breton saga, led on to Sylvie Bizet, a college friend from a small village in another region of Brittanny. Sylvie Two took great delight in our honouring of her celebrated family name. At first she came across as a shy country girl, but she was immensely strong and supportive with Davoren as the trials of adolescence and his second year without his mother took an increasing toll on him. She had a country person's sense of hospitality, which was reciprocated by her being cordially embraced by all the other siblings. Despite the crushing loss of Brighid and increasing anxiety about Davoren's health and failures to communicate, a pattern of warmth and welcoming openness was being established in the house. Davoren with his French 'au pair' became a mecca for schoolfriends and the other helpers. Our home, which could have become a downbeat doleful place, became instead a haven of strange happiness.

□□□□

A surprise telephone call from Theo Dorgan, the director of Poetry Ireland, in late 1990 initiated another buoyant episode in this early period after Brighid's death. Theo wanted Davoren to contribute a poem to something he called *The Great Book of Ireland*. But Theo had also read several poems I had written for Brighid and, to my astonishment, wanted me to contribute something also. Engaged by his infectious Cork enthusiasm, I listened as Theo outlined the idea behind the *Great Book*, which was a hugely imaginative fund-raising project conceived by Clashganna Mills Trust and Poetry Ireland, involving 140 poets and 120 artists and 8 composers working directly on vellum pages. The pages of the book became an arena for dialogue between poets and artists with calligrapher Denis Brown contributing a unifying style. You can think of it as a contemporary Book of Kells with words and images of our time in harmony and contention. In my view it is a neglected modern masterwork.

Clashganna Mills Trust had developed an old mills complex in County Carlow to provide residential and learning facilities and dignity through independent living for people with disabilities. Given that we had also forged very strong links with Poetry Ireland, it was perhaps appropriate that Davoren should have been asked to participate in the *Great Book*. I was frankly embarrassed, however, by Theo's suggestion that I should also contribute, as I had never had a poem published in my life, apart from a special edition brought out for the Bewley's reading after Brighid's death, and I felt that I would be piggy-backing on Davoren. However, after Theo had explained the free-wheeling associations whereby the list of contributors had been built up, I accepted his request.

The *Great Book* had a dizzying effect on me as I swung between lingering embarrassment, raw elation and racking grief. I couldn't help but think that it was a cruel fulfilment of Brighid's dreams for Davoren and myself. One evening after talking to Theo about the project, I left the house barely able to hold myself together; the after-shocks of Brighid's death, even benign ones like the *Great Book*, were still tearing at my heart and guts.

The public unveiling of the *Great Book* took place at the Royal Hospital Kilmainham on 25th June 1991. For Davoren, it was like a re-run of his own book launch in that after the public ceremonial, he was able to bask in the euphoria generated by the realisation of this visionary project. Davoren's effervescence had a strong effect on a friend of mine, Thérèse Hegarty, an innovative teacher with her own family responsibilities, yet who had sustained me greatly after Brighid's death. Thérèse had also very strongly encouraged me to bide my time but persist with my own dream of writing. After the celebration at the RHK, Thérèse came back to Bantry Road. She had rarely seen Davoren in buoyant form — there seemed to be some tension between them — but that evening, the ice was broken as Davoren sat, awkwardly propped up in an ordinary armchair but somehow proudly and triumphantly enthroned. He seemed to beam again with his full radiance. One could well believe him "poised for flight" or "sailing upon a crest of happiness".

But in truth the boy who had written, "poetry laughingly sustains me', had stopped his poetic outpouring, having reached a crisis in his self-expression. He did write some poems after Brighid's death, and there were dramatic bursts of that irrepressible urgency to communicate his vision, but that is what they became in those final years, dramatic peaks. His communication rhythm began to mirror his pattern with me — a lot of frustration, hesitant pointings that were difficult to decipher, and occasional epiphanies.

My conclusions about what was happening for Davoren are no more than fatherly hunches, based on some of what he wrote, reports I received on some of the conversations with his helpers (I would not hear the details of a great many of these conversations nor have I gone around excavating the scraps) and several dramatic incidents.

The overriding themes of Dav's conversations during the last three years of his life were both the farrago of personal anxieties which make up adolescence and his concern for me. Davoren was never spared witnessing the ravages which he wrought on our lives — the night-time traumas were too severe for dissimulation — but now he had witnessed the terrible cost that they had exacted. He knew of — I shared it with him — my resolve to remain hopeful and to find a way forward for both of us but he also knew — I shared these moments too, sometimes not meaning to — my pain and bafflement.

Yet he was carrying the burden of this responsibility for me just at a time when the pressure to forge a separate identity, to break with father-identification, was most intense. As the American essayist Edward Hoagland puts it, "the psychological phenomenon of sons set irremediably against their fathers is not something we are responsible for", so it is pointless to bemoan this elemental wellspring in our natures. Rather sons usually resolve it by staking out their own claim in the world, and thereby distancing themselves (at least temporarily) emotionally from their fathers. Yet if Davoren had by this stage staked a forceful but precarious claim in the world, he was still chronically dependent on me (and the circle of siblings who surrounded us) for every step in his path through life.

One little episode whereby we tried to put a certain psychological distance between us sheds a lot of light on Davoren's state of mind at that time. During the autumn of 1991, I was in touch with Tanya Grandon, the manager of Cuan Aoibhean but also a person experienced in dealing with parents and their handicapped children. Tanya came to see the two of us for a chat and could see clearly that grief over Brighid — instead of loosening its grip on us — was in fact becoming a heavier burden. It was crystal clear to her also that the very intensity of our bond, our capacity to comfort and be playful with each other, masked the fact that we were making it worse for each other. We each missed Brighid terribly in our own ways; we had our own thoughts about her, our memory-medley of sorrow and joy, of guilt and delight. I found Tanya's insights convincing and as Davoren was also enthusiastic, we decided that I would have a few chats with Tanya about issues facing me while she would try to track down someone willing to have a go with Dav.

Tanya subsequently recommended Carmel Byrne, a healer and counsellor working with the Amethyst Centre in Foxrock. On a very hot afternoon I drove Davoren to see Carmel with Tanya present also to make the introductions. We were both very drained when we arrived from stuffiness in the car due to heavy traffic. Nevertheless I was looking forward to introducing Davoren to Carmel. We went into the room where the air of expectation from Carmel and Tanya was palpable. I started to 'explain' Davoren and our history to Carmel, but when I looked over at Davoren in his wheelchair beside me, he was fast asleep.

I was flabbergasted. The stage seemed perfectly set for Davoren — two women hanging on his every smile, frown or tic. I knew he was a difficult 'client' for Carmel with his communication problems but the prospect of her taking on a sleeping Davoren seemed remote. I wanted the ground to open up to swallow me, and mumbling something about my being only the taxi-driver, I left the room to lick my wounds.

When I returned an hour-and-a-half later, I came into a room with the after-glow of animated conversation. Immediately I had left the room, Davoren had become alert and responsive, opening up to Carmel despite his relatively sluggish physical state. Subsequently I brought Davoren out for about five or six sessions with Carmel and a trainee named Giliosa. They lay Davoren down on cushions and did some meditation and relaxation exercises with him using music and holding. After the first meeting, I stayed pretty much outside the sessions but I had a very strong impression that it was an important stage for him. He was away from me and the network of siblings with our expectations and apprehensions; in this sanctuary he didn't have to perform, on a lap or in his chair, rather he could just take in the loving attention of two people who had a healing attitude towards the irreparable loss which had cut into his very marrow.

Carmel didn't report back to me very much and I didn't expect it. However, one impression was indelible: the more time she spent with Davoren, the more she became aware of that powerful will which showed itself on their first meeting; he could shut out the world with an implacable absence or open up to it with a serene and generous presence. He was (and would always remain) radically dependent on others, but there was a depth of self-possession in him which belied this terrible lack of autonomy. Over the years I had ascribed many of Davoren's absences to exhaustion or small fits, little trances he went into, but now I could see more clearly that there was an active self-confinement behind many of these shut-outs.

During the reign of the Sylvies from summer 1991 to summer 1992, Davoren began to experience such terrible pain in his legs that often he would end up screaming in agony. We would have to take him out of his chair and lie him down and work on the legs, or 'nurse' him while soothing the legs also. It was clear sometimes that his shrieks moved from a response to physical pain to a more generalised misery, and it was a strange, cruel relief to us, the witnesses, to see some venting of his grief.

I had a sense of living on a knife-edge and very often as I came home from work in the afternoon (I had by this time transferred to day work with the *Evening Press*), I would be heavy-hearted at the thought of getting through another winter with my own grief and my bafflement at Davoren's dilemma. Sometimes the news from school would be good: he might have had a good session with the art teacher, who used to take him on her lap and get him to indicate colours and shapes for a painting. Or else I would hear that he'd had a severe seizure during English class and had to spend several hours lying down in his den to recover. But invariably there would be a sense of resilience and cheerfulness in the interactions between Davoren, Sylvie and Martyn or whoever else happened to be around.

One of the siblings who did excellent work with Davoren, assuaging his bleakness and lifting his spirits, was Ciara Crawford, who came most Saturday afternoons from the time of Brighid's death. Ciara worked a full week with St Michael's House and had a hectic social life so her commitment to Saturday afternoons was especially appreciated. Some weeks when she arrived with her long curly blonde hair tousled and bedraggled after a particularly late night, I used to ask her to reconsider her undertaking. Ciara had an interest in physiotherapy and over the years had done some training in reflexology, massage and aromatherapy so she often did gentle, soothing work with Davoren on the mat.

Not that he was degenerating into being pampered, for Ciara and her brother also brought him canoeing. And Davoren also finally fulfilled his dream of going fishing with someone who caught real fish when Ciara and her boyfriend Tommy brought him on outings to Howth or Dun Laoghaire.

☐☐☐☐

During that hard winter of 1991-92 with Sylvie, I planned a trip to Brittany for Davoren to visit the Voisin and Bizet families the following June. I invited Martyn to come along as a helper: he had soldiered with Davoren for two years in Rosmini in difficult circumstances, having endured considerable personal stress during that period also, and I felt we would make a good team. The original plan was to go straight to Brittany but with a mix-up in the dates, I decided to include a few days in Paris at the beginning. Moreover I wrote up a description of that Paris trip the following year which gives a good flavour of our lives at that period:

We were an odd trio careering down the Rue de Rivoli at half-one in the morning, having just left the hubbub of the Latin Quarter on the Left Bank. My son, aged seventeen, was laughing convulsively as we chased and sang, enjoying the romance of Paris at night. The Rue de Rivoli was quiet and spacious apart from the occasional Parisian oddity, such as the pair of teenage roller-skaters with whom we nearly collided as we pushed Davoren's wheelchair almost heedlessly on the pavement.

Martyn, a young man of twenty-five with flaming red locks, was just emerging from six barren months. A talented musician, as well as a spellbinder with my speech-locked son, he had a song in his heart that night as he listened to my stories of my student year in Paris. Apart from his family, we were Martyn's closest allies in the world and he was happy to be with us in this city of magic.

My rapture was initially just sheer relief at seeing my son beginning to enjoy himself, for he had been sick and miserable in the Greek restaurant where we had dined earlier. It had seemed like a warm family-style taverna but unfortunately that had just been the street hard-sell to lure us in; once inside the service had been arrogant and inattentive and the food indifferent. I had in fact taken a perverse delight in Davoren's upsetting of the routine of the restaurant.

The night air and buzz of Rue Mouffetard was exhilarating after the clammy embrace of the fake taverna, and so we decided to walk the three or four miles back to the hotel, first through the exotically peopled streets of the Boul' Mich' district and then across the Seine past Notre Dame and the stately municipal buildings of Ile de la Cité. We were a merry, giddy threesome by the time we reached the quieter streets of the Right Bank.

Then, suddenly, I was flooded by another presence in our midst, by memories of other romantic nights in Paris. In truth, we had become a quartet dancing homewards that starry night, our joy pierced with sorrow for Brighid who was with us every step of the way on this pilgrimage. Ever since our year there as students in the early seventies, Paris had become in that famous phrase of Hemingway "a moveable feast". It was like a beacon of hope shining its light down all the years of our life, lending lustre to the good times and deepening the feeling during periods of darker hue. French had become a secret code — and then a not-so-secret one as Davoren twigged our games — during the long years of struggle with his handicap. Long before we ever saw *Casablanca*, we always had Paris to tug at our souls during times of heartbreak.

Of course Paris had not been a benign charming lady of constancy during our time there in the seventies. I had endured some depression and much frustration in my attempts to crack the nut of French philosophy. I had not yet discovered that it was enough to enjoy quarrying for the philosophical stone, even when you knew it could never be found.

In addition Brighid missed her father very much. She knew how lonely he was after her mother's death and how much he missed her. In the end we returned to Ireland rather than stay another year in France, as Brighid had a sense that he might die — which he did, in the spring of the following year.

On a more mundane level, life was often hard, eking out a living on student allowances and student meals. The bureaucracy in French life was horrendous and we missed our friends in Ireland. I remember well being reduced to tears after several encounters with tough Parisians, exclaiming "Paris, you're a bitch." My vehemence surprised me; at that stage in my life, I rarely used strong language. Still in later years we enjoyed playing with the myth of Paris. It was a hymn, a lament, an elegy for our youthful dreams and hopes.

Indeed the ruthless face of Paris had also shown itself on this trip with Davoren. Restaurants were very inhospitable to us, the Metro was almost completely inaccessible and everything seemed to cost a fortune. All these feelings from the past and present had been given a sharp focus for us the previous evening as we wandered around Montmartre. It was a Sunday and there was a carnival atmosphere outside the Sacré Coeur, with jugglers and acrobats, charlatans and sixties-dreamers mingling. Inside the church it had been surprisingly meditative, with powerful singing and passionate preaching from Croatian exiles. Earlier I had shown Davoren the school at Place Clichy where Brighid had been an *assistante* during our year in Paris — a prestigious school for elegant young French girls which sat just a stone's throw from the flesh-and-sex huckstering of the Clichy district.

Foot-weary and hungry by 7.00 pm, we started to look for a restaurant. We were carrying a Moulinex with us to liquidise Davoren's food, and as the restaurants were only beginning to fill up, we anticipated no problems. However, my efforts to explain our requirements to the hostesses and chefs met with a mixture of hostility and incomprehension. Patiently I explained that we did this in Ireland all the time and never encountered any difficulty. Yet they looked at Davoren guiltily and, acknowledging the empty tables, found some excuse or other to turn us away.

I finally cracked at a Chinese restaurant, where a dumb show of refusal by the manager unleashed my pent-up frustration. I let out a torrent of invective about the insult to my son, spitting fury against the French ways of perfectionism and style which excluded him from the Parisian table. I have a good command of French but normally need to be warmed up a little by alcohol or passion for it to flow really fluently. With a mixture of curses and well-chosen phrases, however, I was now transformed into a fierce advocate for the disabled speechless ones. Martyn and Davoren were startled by my ferocity as we left the restaurant. I was proud at having finally fought back against the humiliations we had endured, but at the same time I felt somewhat ashamed and close to tears. I also recalled vividly Brighid's stubborn and angry battles to have Davoren accepted in various places and her sobs of anguish when sometimes she didn't succeed. I had felt her hand and voice strengthening me in my uncharacteristic outburst — indeed my speech had been accompanied by some wild gesticulation.

The café patrons seated at the outside tables were also quite taken aback as this odd threesome/quartet stormed out. We had only gone a few yards down the hill when a cloudburst sent us and the café customers scuttling for cover. We managed to find an alcove close by, which at least protected Davoren from the worst of the downpour. By that time our mood had turned apocalyptic; images of 'shaking the dust from your feet if they do not receive you,' 'summoning the gods to bear witness to the scandal which had been visited upon us' and suchlike fed our giddy euphoria. It seemed 'fitting and just' that the café diners should be scattered in the face of the righteousness of our cause. In truth, our mood wasn't that vengeful; we had moved to finding the whole episode hilarious.

The thunder and lightning were spectacular, the rain ricocheting off the cobbled street and flowing in torrents down the drain channels. We were joined for a short while by another Irish couple who knew us to see from Drumcondra, but they were well-equipped for the elements and after a while moved on, oblivious to our plight. Since we were quite a distance from the car and organising food for Davoren was becoming critical, the humour and bravado of our joust with the restaurant owners of Paris were beginning to wear a little thin.

Then, on the pavement opposite us, a vision appeared. A young woman in a light dress ran barefoot down the street. She was soaked to the skin but seemed oblivious to the torrential rain. It all happened so quickly, like an illusion — but suddenly for us magic was alive and well on the streets of Paris again.

Eventually the rain eased off and I ran back to the car. Damp and cold but nonetheless exhilarated, we drove back to our hotel at Place de la Bastille.

□□□□

As we left Paris, the poppy fields in the plains of central France were another strong reminder of Brighid's presence. The town of Chartres was like an island in the sea of agricultural riches; we visited the cathedral and a little café where the prices were reasonable and the welcome warm; then we were on the road again, confident that the Brittany part of our trip was going to be a success.

Apart from Jane, all of the Breton girls had come to work with Davoren sight unseen, but through some providential blessing, they all had a natural ease and rapport with him. The same held true for their families; throughout the last four years of Davoren's life, we were adopted four-fold in Brittany.

The stress of Parisian inhospitality had taken a toll on Davoren but he quickly recovered his élan around the Voisin and Bizet dinner tables. He shared in tiny sips the Tour de France of regional wines conducted by Jean Voisin, and he also took up the challenge of the call of "Vous venez pour des apéritifs" of Sylvie's grandmother, Marie, a tiny but enormously vigorous woman with a booming voice who was very active in running the family farm. Marie, who had just regained her strength after a hip operation, formed a strong bond with Davoren. She greeted us every morning with a strong, "Bonjour, Davoren. Bonjour, Jack," and kissed him on both cheeks. She had none of that reticence and fear towards him which elderly women in Ireland tended to show.

I, however, found myself in a perplexing in-between stage. On the one hand, despite being a parent, I joined Davoren as his interpreter with Sylvie's young friends. Davoren loved the sound of their voices, the relaxed closeness between the boys and the girls and the warmth of their welcome for this young man who had forged these links between Ireland and Brittany. The freshness and hope of young people overflowed in abundance among this group, like an intensification of the feeling among the 'siblings' back home. Davoren was lapping up the atmosphere but all the time I felt a despairing tug that the odds were stacking up against him. Moreover, the parents of both Sylvie and Jane were at that mature and relaxed stage of marriage when one savours the lingering after-taste of the difficult years of nurture. In the midst of this marital mellowness, I felt very keenly the isolation of being the lone parent destined to carry on the legacy of my son's bewildering gifts.

The final evening in Sylvie's, members of her family came from all the villages in the district to join us at the table. Martyn was in fine musical form, and towards the end of the evening, he sang several songs from 'The Commitments'. Clíona, who had joined us after a few weeks Inter-Railing around Europe, and Sylvie amazed us as authentic Commitmentettes. Sylvie's parents joined us in some rock 'n' roll and Marie, a life-long member of the local church choir, sang a moving evocation of France's wartime agonies.

Nourishment Nemesis

Taking up the reins of everyday living in Bantry Road after our Breton frolics was a rude shock. There was no disguising Davoren's frailty and lack of stamina and the care arrangements were also precarious, so that we were right up against a host of problems. But there was a short lull before the storm as I had earlier planned a week's break for myself in late June 1992, doing a residential course with Judith Ashton by the banks of the Liffey near Newbridge, Co Kildare. It turned out to be one of the best holidays of my life — massage, counselling, music and swimming three and four times a day in the river. Also attending Judith's course was Margaret Gleeson, a former pianist with the RTÉ Concert Orchestra. She gave the evenings in Barrettstown House a special atmosphere, playing the piano as the light faded with the murmur of the Liffey flowing by in the background. Margaret had been widowed after a marriage of twenty years just a few months after Brighid's death. We had a lot more in common than that — not least jumping into water at any time of the day or night — and we became very close.

I told Margaret all about Davoren, and she claims I wept as I told how our visit to Paris had reawakened my youthful dreams of my life with Brighid. She had followed his progress in the newspapers and on television, even though her own life had been very traumatic at the time when *Poised for Flight* was broadcast. Intrigued, she was very much looking forward to meeting him. Her own words, written to me after his death, best describe her reactions on first seeing him in the flesh:

> You brought me into his bedroom and said, "This is my son." I saw a pair of blazing eyes and a thick shock of hair. Then I felt something like a body-blow as I noticed the extent of his physical disability. He and I gazed at each other for a long, still, silent

161

extraordinary moment. I held my breath and to my horror, the body-blow feeling just kept on increasing until I had a profound sense of loss, as if his disability had actually become mine. I was riveted to the floor. The next instant he gave me a lop-sided grin and made a welcoming sound. My goose was cooked. I felt completely at home.

While he was in respite care during my week's holiday, the crisis over Davoren's feeding intensified. Despite long hours spent 'shovelling' by staff, he lost a lot of weight. A few weeks later he was hospitalised with severe anaemia and an inability to fight infection. It was the first occasion on which he was given blood transfusions.

The truth was that, even when all the resources of those who knew his patterns intimately were brought into play, feeding him was becoming more and more an uphill struggle. When I was feeding him or looking on (which could be far harder), I often thought he must be consuming more energy with the coughing and choking than he could possibly be taking in from the little food he managed to absorb. More food ended up spattered around the room or on the kitchen roll which we used as a napkin ('kitchen roll' was the first new English word learned by all the Breton girls) than in his stomach. He would be completely exhausted after a two-hour spooning session. It was becoming a vicious circle with him not having enough energy to climb the mountain of another meal.

Apart from Davoren's feeding fight to survive, the other main trauma in our lives was that the French connection seemed to have broken down. By dint of several stressful makeshift arrangements, we got through the summer months of 1992, but with the start of the new school year in September I had to make a definite contract with someone if the twenty-four-hour care that Davoren required at home was to continue. By this time I was working only a three-day week with the *Evening Press* by special arrangement, but it was still an exhausting schedule as I took special responsibility for getting up with Davoren during the night. It was only in extreme emergencies that I called on the au pairs to help me out during the middle of the night and, fortunately for them, they all had an ability to sleep through Davoren's normal distress signals.

I decided that the blessing which the girls from Brittany had bestowed on our household, that exotic dimension they brought to 'Dav's harem,' was at an end and somewhat reluctantly I advertised for help locally. However, a few weeks later, I received a telephone call from Guénaëlle Havy, who came from a village near Sylvie Bizet's in the heart of Brittany. From what Sylvie had told her about us, Guénaëlle seemed to be already in love with Davoren. Twenty-six, she was keen to take a career break from academic research, but her positive enthusiasm for coming to stay with us far outweighed any incidental reasons she may have had for taking an 'au pair' job in Ireland. All of this came through vividly in our first phone conversation.

I was in deep conflict, having already made a new and positive arrangement for Davoren's home care but also sensing very strongly a chain of destiny, linking Guénaëlle, Davoren and myself, in this call from Brittany. A few weeks later, however, circumstances changed in Davoren's care arrangements, and I got back on the phone to Guénaëlle immediately to discover that she was still available and keen to join us.

Thus began a friendship for Davoren which was to mark him deeply until his death. Guénaëlle matched all our expectations. She was charming and elegant but also very solid and down-to-earth. Light-hearted and witty, she had alongside that a deeply reflective and sensitive nature. Her English was excellent but sufficiently at an angle to normal usage (sometimes deliberately so) to make it refreshing. She quickly fell into her own style of irreverence towards the pieties and traditions of the household. Most importantly of all, the love for Davoren which I had detected on the phone was no passing show. His difficulties were intensifying all the time but Guénaëlle and he met in a "heart-bonding" which vanquished all hardships. In Breton the name Guénaëlle means 'white angel' and that she truly was in crossing our threshold at that time.

What's more, Guénaëlle's world was turned upside-down in more ways than one by her coming to Bantry Road. On her first weekend with us, she went out to a céilí with some of the other siblings where she met Clíona and Sorcha's brother, Colm Saidléar. A relationship slowly developed which gave rise to many nights seated brooding by the hearth as she wondered what this sojourn in Ireland had in store for her. After living with us for twelve months, she stayed on in Ireland with Colm, continuing the connection with Davoren at first informally and then working with the Center for Independent Living, a network organised by handicapped people themselves to train and employ personal assistants.

If I thought I had a crisis before Guénaëlle's arrival, it was nothing to the anguish I suffered when the time came for her to move on. I knew we were not losing her entirely but I felt a terrible heaviness at the thought of this constant moving on to new people. Fortunately, a totally different angel fell out of the sky into our lives. Céline (from *ciel* meaning sky) Tessier was from St Pol de Léon, a town near Roscoff, a port on the north coast of Finistèrewhich many Bretons regard as true Brittany. Céline, with her mass of tumbling curls and large startled brown eyes, was proud of her Finistèreconnections, but in truth was a citizen of the world.

Céline was so defiantly and elegantly herself that there was never any question of invidious comparisons with the special qualities of Guénaëlle. In fact, with Guénaëlle still in close contact with us, they became very close friends. Céline was warm, bright, bushy-tailed and efficient. She entered into the increasingly difficult situation at our home with barely a flicker of her long eyelashes over her lustrous brown eyes. Experiencing frequent bouts of pain from his ulcer and spells of listlessness, Davoren often needed to be comforted, and if he had filled out somewhat, he could still be cradled comfortably in the embrace of a Breton girl. Céline also stepped into the *mère poule* role with a couple of her French friends and often joked that she went from comforting Davoren during the day to consoling her fellow au pairs in the evening.

Our Breton 'extended family' also caused a new spark across the generations between my father and Davoren. While his mental faculties were as sharp as ever, his sight and hearing were failing as he crossed the threshold of his nineties. However, he invariably brightened up in the presence of the Breton charm of Jane, Sophie (as he always mistakenly referred to Sylvie), Janelle (his best shot at Guénaëlle) and Céline. He had some little French which he liked to throw into the chat about French life and politics. The girls' evident appreciation and natural acceptance of Davoren and his chirpy response in turn had a markedly warming effect on my father's attitude towards Davoren. He could see clearly what a draw Dav was for these remarkable young people who gathered around him from home and abroad.

◻◻◻◻

During the autumn of 1992, the casualty department and wards of Beaumont Hospital had become a regular port of call as a diagnosis of bleeding from his oesophagus was added to Davoren's chronic risk of pneumonia from the inhalation of food into his lungs. Nevertheless, he still showed a great capacity to bounce back — this was after all the first year of Guénaëlle — and there was a new impetus in school with Denis Dermody rounding off the roll of honour of school helpers.

Denis was a particularly inspired candidate for a role in Davoren's life during this time of transition to adulthood, as his whole approach was to take the lead from the handicapped person with whom he worked. In the gentlest possible way, he forced me to come to terms with Davoren making decisions about his own life. In theory I recognised the importance of this but in practice I often slipped into carrying the responsibility for his decisions (and thereby taking it away from him) since I was already carrying the responsibility for so much in his life.

The best example of Denis's style concerned something which, if trivial, can often loom large in relations between fathers and sons — Davoren's wish to have his ear pierced. Hints began to be dropped around this time about Davoren's interest in an earring, as various siblings with different methods of communicating with him came back with the same report. I was evasive, mostly rehearsing my own generation's distaste for such adornments and also reckoning that Davoren had enough piercing in his life already. Usually I tried to fob him off with the same old ploy my father used when a request was made — "We'll see." Whereas in my father's case this was usually a prelude to the request being granted, I hoped that the issue would just go away. I certainly wasn't going to bring him to get his ear pierced and I thought none of the siblings would either, without express authorisation.

One afternoon on a day off from school, Denis brought Davoren into town and he came home with the job done. If I'd ever had any doubts about Davoren's stubborn independence of mind, his smile of triumph that day would have dispelled them. Denis had been full of apprehension on two fronts: first about my reaction, and secondly because he was terrified of Davoren screaming when the ear was being pierced. At that stage he hadn't had much experience with Davoren on the hospital shift where Davoren was often stoical as a doctor spent an hour trying to get a good line into his shallow childlike veins. In fact Denis reported that Dav had just blinked with mild surprise. I never became enthusiastic about the earring and, when it wasn't on him, often managed to ensure that it got mislaid, yet I never held it against Denis.

Just before Christmas in 1992, Davoren was again in hospital. After an abortive attempt to examine Davoren's oesophagus by inserting a tube containing a camera down his throat, the doctors wanted permission to give him an anaesthetic. With Davoren's breathing problems and history of chest infections, doctors were very wary of submitting him to too many general anaesthetics. However they were also strongly recommending inserting a PEG feeding tube into his stomach, if the problems with the oesophagus turned out to be acute. The doctors' overall opinion was that Davoren's feeding problems had become so acute that without the PEG tube (which goes directly through the stomach wall at waist level), he would not get sufficient nourishment to sustain himself.

This advice led on to a flurry of consultations between Davoren and myself, between Davoren and his communication helpers and between me and anyone I thought could advise me. I was very agitated about the whole business, as I felt it as a terrible failure after sixteen-and-a-half years of feeding him. There was, however, a funny side to my anxieties as the siblings noticed on several occasions my diving for cover beside Davoren's bed at the approach of three female registrars who needed to get a decision from me. Davoren and the siblings laughed heartily at my quailing in terror in the face of "the three witches". In fact the doctors were exemplary in dealing with me and Davoren, explaining the options and respecting our decisions, and I had the greatest of respect for them. Finally I gave my consent.

Still, I never fully adapted to the idea of pouring food into Davoren, and I went off cooking for some considerable time, even though Davoren had never eaten my meals except as liquidised pap. Davoren himself was philosophical. "At last my long battle with food is over" or afterwards "Jack is dealing fabulously with my tube," he wrote in conversations with Sorcha, making jokes about beans and sausages.

On the afternoon before the operation, Davoren was in very perky form. As I learned only a long time afterwards, Denis dressed him up for outdoors and with the permission of the ward sister, brought him out for a walk. They ended up in Beaumont House, where Davoren had a hot port. He sailed through the operation the following day, as was the case indeed with all the surgical procedures he underwent during his life.

On Christmas Eve he was discharged from hospital with a supply of cans of concentrated liquid food for his festive fare. He didn't seem to mind at all as with my brother and his family, Guénaëlle and I tucked into our Christmas dinner. Despite his blessing, I couldn't help feeling a bit guilty.

◻◻◻◻

In early January 1993, before the resumption of school, we decided to make a trip down to our old friends in Connemara, Barbara and Dave Hogan, then living in Cleggan with their two sons, Kevin and toddler Brian. All three of us, Davoren, Guénaëlle and I, had been through a tough time and I thought we needed a lift for the New Year. I can still hear the voice of my father saying "clown" as he contemplated the folly of bringing this "invalid child" (as he saw Davoren) just out of hospital down to the wilds of north Connemara. Even at ninety, my father still had the power to intimidate but in this case I knew my instincts were sound. A warm welcome, music and conviviality awaited us even if Davoren could not scale the same peaks as during the great Letterfrack Christmas of

1984. Happily we had the same kind of weather, cold sunny days with crisp moonlit nights. We didn't stay with Barbara and Dave on the hills overlooking Cleggan Bay but in cottages out on Cleggan Head. The few days in the West gave us a chance to settle into a new routine to build Davoren up for his eighteenth birthday.

I was forced to admit that the PEG tube was very successful initially. Davoren filled out a lot, lost his aura of fragility and the frightening whiteness of his complexion. He also went into a late teenage bloom of acne which upset him a lot. In any case we celebrated his eighteenth birthday with gusto. By this time parties were becoming a bit of an institution among Davoren's gang.

His graduation from Rosmini in 1993 was a bit of an anti-climax as his future was now very uncertain. Despite immense goodwill from Rosmini and from Department of Education officials, Davoren was not able to participate in the Leaving Certificate rite of passage. Everyone was willing to bend over backwards to accommodate him, while maintaining the integrity of the exam, but his communication problems had become too severe and in any case I could not get helpers to work with him for the length of time that would be required. Helplessly and ruefully I looked back on the battles with the educational authorities which Brighid had waged over many years on behalf of Davoren.

During the spring of 1993, I began reading Brian Keenan's *An Evil Cradling* with Davoren. We found it a riveting, if somewhat harrowing, read, even though Brian steers away from wallowing in the brutality of his captors. One evening when we were alone in the house, I started a new chapter in which Brian reflects on the notion of an 'oubliette' — a dungeon into which prisoners were thrown and forgotten. I was holding Davoren on my lap, when suddenly there was a very strong reaction from him, and I felt a terrible chill myself. What Brian wrote — "Those who resided in our oubliette will not easily forget it, even if in time the world shall forget." — matched so perfectly the place into which Davoren's 'voice' with all its soaring and searing truths seemed to have fallen. On such Saturday nights, the two of us felt completely abandoned and, like Brian Keenan and his fellow hostages, it was only occasional flashes of humour and mad antics that kept us from despair.

Yet that night I typed with Davoren, who worked with strong vigorous sweeps of his arms as it was urgent that he communicate. I still wasn't the most adept person in the world at following his directions but I had no difficulty in getting a few sentences out of him. Unfortunately I have lost the record of the conversation: all I remember is that he wanted to make a defiant assertion of freedom in the face of darkness and forgetfulness.

We were not left for long in our oubliette however, as later that spring a team of builders descended on us to construct the long-awaited extension for Davoren. There had been a few technical hitches in the implementation of the Woodie's plan to build the special day-room for Davoren, but once an executive named Simon Thornton took charge, everything proceeded smoothly. The chaos, noise and dust from the gutting of our cramped spaces at the back of the house were very disruptive but the cheerful vigour and friendliness of the building crew more than compensated. These were men who were proud of their work and happy that it was going to make a difference to Davoren's life.

We held an all-day house-warming party on 4th July, which turned out to be the best of all our parties. In a way, just three years after Brighid's death, it was a powerful affirmation of vibrant life continuing on at Bantry Road, and we gave thanks.

Music Hungers for Hearing

I will measure out a tune
for you with my folded fists.

The sound of his mother's heart-beat had no doubt awakened a response in the foetally hunched Davoren. Later Brighid's voice had stirred baby Davoren to smile, and then her hearty encouragement had pushed him to make his own 'little sound'. Indeed his most powerful voicings had been achieved linked heart-to-heart with her, until that great heart stopped beating and he'd had to find his sound again.

As well as being rocked into life by these primordial rhythms, Davoren also had a life of immersion in composed music and music-making. As I mentioned earlier, that exposure had begun in the womb, as he listened to Mozart's symphonies during the weeks Brighid spent lying in bed at a critical stage during the pregnancy. In any case it was certainly clear very early on that he had an extraordinarily acute ear for sound.

When Brighid was asked to recount the story of her awareness of Davoren's intelligence, she invariably went back to the milestone of his first smile, which appeared within the normal span according to the baby books. For myself, I always go back to music, in particular to his trance-like response to a signature tune for a programme called 'The Music Box' on RTÉ radio at the time. 'The Music Box' is a short waltz by Shostakovich played on strings. It used to have an extraordinary effect on Davoren, who only had to hear the first bar of the tune for a spaced-out look to appear on his face. Later as Brighid sang it or played it on various instruments around the house, the same effect could be seen. There were other unusual responses to sound: tiny background noises like the clicking on or off of the fridge or of something small being dropped, sounds which were barely audible above the general hubbub, would evoke very strong reactions.

Along with these initial observations, Davoren asserted his desire to write music very early on in his communications. "Music weaves its notes through my blood like light weaves through the universe. Definitely I want to be more prolific as a composer when I master the computer," he wrote at a time when he still had hopes of using a computer for his writing. In fact he often used to say that his real dream was to write an opera rather than poetry. He had even chosen a theme for a children's opera based on Oscar Wilde's story, 'The Fisherman and His Soul'. As his difficulties in communicating at all were almost insuperable, you can imagine the moonshot involved in helping him to write music. Nevertheless try Brighid and himself did, and there are fragments scattered through the files of methods devised for him to choose his notes, the intervals and the rhythm. Included in these scraps is a love duet for his proposed children's opera.

Thus, when in the early summer of 1993 I received information about a music and drama workshop for people with disabilities, I seized on it as a possible stimulus to revitalize Davoren. The organisation involved was Share Music, a group set up by Dr Michael Swallow, a retired neuro-surgeon living in Belfast. They were keen to have Davoren, provided I was able to send a suitable helper with him.

Guénaëlle, who was spending the summer with us, was keen to try something new with Davoren. She had a strong background in music, having sung in a choir while at university. Given her sensitive rapport with Davoren, Guénaëlle had been a prime candidate for typing with him and had made many attempts, but between a mixture of affection getting in the way, lack of clarity from Davoren and Guénaëlle's doubts about her English, all they had achieved up to that point was "a goo of letters". Meanwhile Margaret Gleeson, who was retraining to work as a music therapist, was very interested in the course and contacted Michael Swallow about helping out. In the event, such was the pressure of Davoren's activities, she was press-ganged into being a full-time back-up to Davoren and Guénaëlle.

The course took place in the middle of August at the Share Centre on the shores of Upper Lough Erne near Lisnaskea in Co Fermanagh. I dropped Davoren and Guénaëlle off on my way to Donegal with Clíona to do some work on the cottage. The arrangement was that I would come back and stay the night for the final evening's performance. The course tutors were adamant from the word go that everything for the show had to originate from the group so the workshop started with a buzz-session on themes and plots. Guénaëlle reported to me that Davoren was very low-key for two or three days. Others seemed to be more assertive and forthcoming with ideas and had more straightforward ways of making their 'voices' heard. It was possibly a new experience for him to find himself in the background in a mill of fellow handicapped people bursting with creative ideas. But the course tutors and helpers pushed all the participants very hard; there could be no opting out.

The story chosen by the group dealt with a reversal of fortunes between a rich and powerful elite and a downtrodden group living on a sunny island. The oppressed people contributed colour, music and dance to the medley of life. Their possession of true riches was revealed when the oppressors fell to pieces after a great storm cut them off from their wealth.

On the third day, during a break from the creative work, there was a 'Banana Boat' trip on Lough Erne. The colourful boat, the exuberant sing-along and a strong breeze blowing into their faces made it an exciting voyage. Guénaëlle remembers the moment very precisely. All the participants were in the same boat at the end, with tears in their eyes from the lacerating wind as they came ashore. When they got back to the warmth of their room, Davoren suddenly sprang to life. He wanted to make a words and music contribution and it had to be done immediately. Guénaëlle had never seen anything like it. From then until the end of the week, Dav relentlessly drove Guénaëlle, Margaret and anyone else he could enlist — typing, writing out his music and dancing, which involved Guénaëlle lifting him out of his chair and jigging around with him over her shoulder.

But it was not just a burst of manic energy. Rather there was a precision about his movements, his pointing to the letters, his naming of the notes, his specifying of the intervals: all unlike any previous working experience she'd had with him.

> It was like he was on his own and I was just an instrument. He wanted to dance all the time. It was as if there was no physical restriction, no limit on his energy. It was amazing. That week he carried me.

The basic melody he wanted was hammered out insistently in about five minutes, after which Margaret and Guénaëlle set about asking him detailed questions about timing and stress. His words and music were tightly woven into the plot of the group story, Davoren's particular theme being "Sadness is deeper without music."

I arrived back from my Donegal excursion to find a very excited and exhausted trio. There was barely time during the hectic schedule to pour a can of food down his tube. At the end of a long day when Guénaëlle and Margaret were ready to drop, Davoren was still bursting with energy, and he had become much more open to all the participants and helpers on the workshop.

The performance took place in a barn-like structure with huge paintings, done using the wheelchairs, as backdrops. This work had been carried out to pulsating samba rhythms which had put Guénaëlle to flight, but Davoren couldn't have enough of it as he and Margaret made their mark. The performance was colourful, inventive and dynamic, and with the help of a very resourceful music technology team led by Michelle McCormack from Newry, many of the participants were able to perform their own music, using light beams and other devices. Davoren's song was sung very movingly by a young music student from England who was helping on the course.

An all-night party followed with Davoren's pal, Stephen Olwill, and his brothers in the thick of it; Davoren, Margaret and I eventually conked out. A very dishevelled but happy troupe returned to Dublin the next day.

August optimism did not however yield an autumn harvest, as in late September Davoren was rushed to hospital with what turned out to be a very severe liver disorder. I had minded him at home by myself for several days before admission to hospital, so I think I was already punch-drunk by the time we reached the casualty department in Beaumont. Davoren was very weak and looked ghastly, so I stayed with him and tried to reassure him as best I could while the usual round of poking at him with needles began. The attention we got in an overstretched casualty department was as usual excellent. After an hour or two Margaret Gleeson joined us, and sang and talked gently to Davoren. Margaret had developed a very close bond with Davoren, especially over the week in Lisnaskea. At some stage, while I took a break, she sensed that Davoren was frightened. Through a series of questions, she teased out of him that he thought he was dying and that he was afraid.

For several days he remained critical and wasn't responding to treatment. After consulting with a friend, Margaret contacted Fr Dara Molloy, who had assisted so sensitively at the funeral ceremonies for Brighid. Dara said he would come straight away from his Inis Mór community on the Aran Islands. After several anxious days, Davoren pulled out of the crisis and then received an additional boost from a visit by Brighid's brother, Brendan, back in Ireland for a few days from Australia. Nevertheless he was only beginning to pick up when Margaret, Dara, Gary and myself gathered for the Sacrament of the Sick in the private room he'd been given because of fears that his liver complications might have been due to hepatitis.

Davoren was in a trance of wide-eyed attentiveness throughout the ceremony, sitting steadily and serenely in his wheelchair. Dara explained beautifully the various components of the rite, the origin of the oils and the various blessings. In fact we all felt privileged to be in attendance. At the end Gary took Davoren on his lap in front of the letter-board, expecting to get a few weak responses from him. Instead a sparkling light shone from Davoren's eyes and he engaged in a lengthy dialogue with Dara. We could not believe that this dynamic rag-doll on Gary's knee was the same person who a week earlier had been at the threshold of death.

❑❑❑❑

That numbed state which had afflicted me in the casualty department of Beaumont unfortunately remained a very frequent companion as we struggled through our fourth winter and spring after Brighid's death. Around February and March in particular I spent long hours at night holding him with his chest heaving alarmingly as he gasped for breath. As his whole chest went into a concave spasm, I was never very sure that it would fill out again. Once or twice I had terrible flashbacks to Brighid's death and thought that he was about to die in my arms as she had done. Mostly however, I got through it by shutting down, sleepwalking emotionally, especially if it was the third or fourth such call during the night.

What was happening became dramatically clear to me once or twice at a bio-energetics class run by Mary Arthurs that I attended that spring. Bio-energetics focuses on breathing and the flow of energy throughout the whole body; it puts the spotlight of awareness on how deep issues in our lives affect our whole posture and stance. That spring at the classes I would suddenly become aware of what had been happening to me the previous night — the terror of his dying in my arms and my prayers for help for us both, and, in honesty, the hope that maybe he would slip away peacefully to end the torture shadowing his every breath. The distress in his eyes from his gulping struggles to stay alive was often an unbearable sight: like being condemned to watch interminably that struggle for a first breath by a new-born baby. Away from the house, the tensions of those night-time vigils would re-inhabit my body at Mary Arthurs' class, where I would shake and shudder, until gradually the stress would ease away from me and I would find a kind of peace.

Grieving Feathers

I heard his cry
and saw the glint of hope
in his grieving feathers.

Dating from his almost-miraculous renaissance on that giddy late April afternoon in 1994, Davoren sailed upon the crest of a strong, steady, gentle wave during May and June. Brittany still remained a beacon of hope for us, and as Céline was due to go back to France at the end of June, I began to put out feelers to all my contacts in Brittany that there would be a vacancy coming up in the by-now celebrated Davoren Hanna household.

Now that his physical strength and spirits had improved, I felt more optimistic about finding a new person to work with Davoren despite the fact that his daily routine was still very unstructured. When he had finished school, the scheme for his school helper had also been terminated. Davoren then linked up with the Center for Independent Living, who organised a personal assistant for him. This fledgling organisation had all the chaos and hand-to-mouth funding that you would expect but there was a wonderful spirit behind it. Davoren had found it hard to mix in with the tougher, more independent people in the CIL, particularly as it had been such a rough time for him physically, but in general it was a positive new departure in his life.

His time in Cuan Aoibhean (5th July to 19th July) gave me an opportunity to redouble my efforts to set up structures for the rest of the summer and the following year. I brought him home for the evening on 8th July for a quiet gathering to honour Brighid's anniversary. Davoren sat in his wonderful new room at the back of the house underneath Veronica Bolay's painting in memory of Brighid, 'For the Poppy Woman'. On the table in front of him, a large spray of multi-coloured freesia added a lovely scent to the room. The sun was setting at the back of the house as we chatted in the gentle evening light and I brought Davoren back to Cuan Aoibhean in a peaceful frame of mind.

A more hectic gathering was planned for the following Friday evening. Davoren's former teacher and now friend, Barry Gleeson, was launching his CD, *Path across the Ocean*, at the Góilín Singers' Club in the upstairs lounge of the Trinity Bar in Pearse Street. My car was stolen in the afternoon but that didn't bother me too much. After many years of 'bangers' which nobody would bother to steal, I had had my car taken several times and another good car had gone up in flames while I was driving it, so I was becoming philosophical about cars and would in fact have been much more upset had my bicycle been stolen.

Margaret Gleeson (no relative of Barry's) and I collected Davoren at Cuan Aoibhean, then joined Martyn Mulhere and Denis Dermody in the pub. We had attended the Góilín Club several times and knew many of the regulars, so there was a warm welcome for Davoren, whose old friends, the Voice Squad, were also there. It wasn't a normal launch, as there was to be a complete evening of music and singing. Barry had put a huge amount of work into preparing the CD and the Góilín gang were delighted for him.

Unfortunately it was a sweltering evening and the venue so packed that the atmosphere in the lounge was stifling. I decided I would drop up to Pearse Street Garda station to see if there was any news about my car, which had been found, undamaged apart from the ignition, door and steering locks.

I went back to the Trinity Bar where Margaret and I decided to collect the car and bring it home. I was a bit apprehensive about leaving Davoren in the pub because of the heat and lack of air, Margaret having already been forced to retreat to the stairs. Nevertheless he was in good company, enjoying the pub atmosphere even if he couldn't join in the drinking.

When I returned about an hour later and felt the blast of heat in the room, I expected at the very least that he would be slumped with exhaustion. Instead I found him seated between Martyn and Denis, stripped to his tee-shirt with his feeding tube dangling out, looking a sight but very perky. Even though it was near closing time, there was no let-up in the party and I felt an awful spoil-sport when I suggested we should begin to make tracks back to the Phoenix Park, where I was worried about the staff having to settle him down for the night.

Davoren didn't hold it against me — most of the time he enjoyed these father-and-son games — and was in high, croaking form as Margaret drove us through the Phoenix Park. Cuan Aoibhean is a single-storey relatively modern building at the back of the main complex in St Mary's Hospital. Just as we turned the final corner towards Cuan Aoibhean, Margaret's headlights picked out three deer standing in front of a blank white wall. Two of them were sitting down but the third stood staring at us with his full array of antlers dramatically lit up and shadowed on the wall. We lifted Davoren up in his seat to see. The deer just stayed where they were, contemplating us contemplating them.

Within Cuan Aoibhean, nearly all the residents were asleep and the night staff were doing some routine work. We gave Davoren some food through his tube and tried to restrain his shouting. His eyes were sparkling and he was letting out whoops of delight, even though it was now well after midnight. As we left him, his cries of happiness were still echoing down the corridor.

⬜⬜⬜⬜

Martyn brought Davoren to a Center for Independent Living meeting on Saturday and reported that Davoren participated much more in the discussions. Everyone remarked how much more open he seemed.

Since they were running out of cans of Davoren's food in Cuan Aoibhean, I was intending to call up with supplies. However Guénaëlle was in contact with me, saying she and Colm had the Saidléar car for the evening and so they would save me the trip. Davoren was sitting serenely in the dayroom when they arrived and Guénaëlle spent some quiet time with him, with a few giggles thrown in for good measure.

⬜⬜⬜⬜

That week had been a very active one in the Hanna family, as my father, who had been ninety-two in May, was declining rapidly. Despite chronic emphysema for over twenty-five years, he had held onto a high degree of independence, living at home with my brother David. My other two brothers, Peter and Paul, with their wives Mary and Joan, had provided considerable support for him at home and a nurse called occasionally. I had been excused most of the routine back-up because of Davoren and because I lived that bit farther away, though I tried to compensate by calling for longer chats.

Yet the system was now breaking down, with my father getting confused and falling quite frequently. He'd already had several bad falls and the strain on David was becoming intolerable. A full-time rota of nurses in the house or a nursing home were the only options. After several family meetings, the job of finding a suitable nursing home was delegated to my sister-in-law Mary. She had in fact found an excellent home where he would be accepted as soon as there was a vacancy. In the meantime other members of the family were providing a back-up for David during the night.

I volunteered to do the weekend nights of 16th and 17th July, even though my father was adamantly opposed to my staying the night as he argued that I had enough on my plate with Davoren. There had already been a huge row when David inadvertently let slip that I had gone for a swim on the Saturday afternoon. I thought he would die of apoplexy in the bed, as he considered that I was so worn down with Davoren (true enough) that I wasn't able for swimming. The truth was that it was activities like swimming and running that kept me balanced.

David and I agreed that I would stay the night but without letting on that I was there. I would only appear if there was a real emergency. So I spent most of the weekend skulking about the house with occasional visits to Margaret Gleeson who lived nearby. The World Cup final from the US was on television on the Sunday night. I was keenly aware that Brighid had died just after the conclusion of the final in Italy four years previously. Given that awareness and the poor quality of the play, I took only a desultory interest in the football.

It was an eerie feeling spending my first nights back at my family home since I had left to get married more than twenty-four years previously. I slept fitfully enough with my father shouting for David several times during the night, thinking it was time to get up. I could hear David calmly reasoning with him, never an easy thing to do, yet David eventually persuaded him to settle down again.

At 7.30 on Monday morning I left for work and to resume my life on the north side of the city. I was reasonably calm about Davoren coming home on Tuesday, even though I had not fixed up any new au pair yet. However, Cuan Aoibhean had been in touch with the subs' desk at the *Press* even before 8 o'clock when they couldn't get me at home. I rang them and was told that Davoren was very critical, and that it was urgent I get up there. While I was very frightened, I only dimly suspected that Davoren might be dying.

When I got to Cuan Aoibhean, the sister brought me into the office and told me it was the worst possible news. Davoren had passed away peacefully in his sleep at 7.20 that morning. He had been observed breathing easily and regularly by a passing nurse shortly before. When he was checked again at 7.20, the nurse noticed that he had stopped breathing. All their efforts to resuscitate him had failed. The doctor who certified his death had put down cardiac respiratory arrest as the cause of death. I was entitled to ask for a post mortem but there did not seem to be any point. Davoren had been in great form all day Sunday. In fact the staff at Cuan Aoibhean were delighted that his stay had gone so well. As such his death was a terrible shock to them.

I cried tears of wretchedness and then grew calm, a pattern that went on for a while. I then went down to see Davoren, who had a ghostly pallor but otherwise looked very peaceful. After praying with the staff, I knelt on the floor beside his bed and hugged and kissed him. After a cup of tea I started to make some phone calls — to Margaret, to Guénaëlle and to my family. I then walked about in the long grass outside Cuan Aoibhean, fisting the air and pleading with the skies while I waited for someone to come.

Epilogue: Poised for Flight

Davoren's grave is in Fingal Cemetery off the Malahide Road. It is a new graveyard, busy with people tending the graves of their loved ones. There are a surprising number of young people buried there, the headstones very showy and effusive. There's nothing there to my taste but I enjoy its aliveness. I like to spend time there if it's not too cold — to potter around Davoren's grave while other families potter around theirs.

Davoren's grave is still marked by a simple wooden cross which I made myself. A friend of Ciara's burned his name, his dates and 'Poised for Flight' into the wood. It was the only thing I could think of at the time. For his first anniversary I had a good show of flowers. Now that this book is written I will go about finding some suitable Burren or Clare stone to put on his grave.

◻◻◻◻

The days following Davoren's death were themselves very moving. Even though in a sense Davoren's story was over, his spirit presided very powerfully over those days. We decided to bring his body back for a vigil in the house, where he was laid out in his fancy shirt, his leather waistcoat and black jeans. He looked serene and at times you could almost imagine his cheeky grin defiantly shining out from his immobility. There were lots of candles and fragrant flowers. Several generations of siblings called and friends and relatives: it was an evening of prayer and laughter, of tears and stories.

The moment of Gary's arrival summed it up best. Gary was always a large, unignorable presence. On this occasion he came in quietly and stood before the coffin and talked non-stop for about an hour — hilarious stories, some of which we had heard before, some new, stories about the tough times and how this little guy had shaken up his life. Gary and his

181

wife Gráinne had just had a little baby boy, Eoin, who was about a month old. He was a beautiful presence around the house all evening — wide-eyed new life in the midst of the passing away of a young life fully lived. As the evening drew in, the atmosphere grew even more peaceful. The doors to the garden were open and people passed in and out, as Davoren lay in the flickering candlelight.

I slept on the floor beside the coffin that night. It was like the night up in the cottage on my own after Brighid's death — time to let it sink in a little. Joe Dunne slept upstairs. Again around six o'clock I began to go a little crazy but I didn't feel the need to disturb Joe. That was part of it too.

⬚⬚⬚⬚

That afternoon we carried Davoren's body to the church, up and down the little Drumcondra roads he walked so often in his wheelchair, the siblings taking it in turns to put a shoulder to the coffin. Dara Molloy had again come from Aran with Tess Harper, another member of the island community, to lead the ceremonies. At the removal service, Barbara Callan, who had just arrived from Connemara, sang a song she had written in Irish honouring St Brigid and the Brigid goddess of mythology — with some verses hinting at the mighty Brighid who had been such a part of Davoren's life. I quote just one verse:

> *A Mháthair Mhór, i do chuideachta*
> *Ta brí is aoibhneas i mo chroí.*
> *Led' sholas corcra treoraíonn tú mé*
> *Ar bhealach gheal mo shaoil.*
> *Is tú a spreagas mé chun ceoil*
> *'S an file chun a dhánta.*
> *Is tusa foinse na fáistine*
> *Bíodh beannacht ortsa go deo.*
>
> *Great Mother, in your company*
> *My heart is full of strength and joy.*
> *With your purple light you guide me*
> *On the bright road of my life.*
> *It's you who move me to my song*

Epilogue: Poised for Flight

And the poet to his poems.
You are the spring of prophecy,
May you be blessed for ever.

At the funeral Mass the next day, various elements of Davoren's life were woven into the service. His letter-board, his book and his earring were among the offertory gifts. Nóirin Ní Riain sang, moving flowingly around his coffin, her voice plunging and soaring in a way that echoed Davoren's life. Guénaëlle spoke beautifully in French of the Breton bonding. Niamh Digan read one of his Irish poems. Margaret Gleeson's brother, David Mac Kenzie, played the meditation from Thais by Massenet on the violin, a piece we often used for quiet contemplative times. Martyn played on the guitar. Poems and prayers were read by siblings and cousins, including one by his cousin Ken Woods who had just flown in from Perth.

I had thought I would not be able to take part in the ceremonies in the crowded church, but the previous evening I had written a little reflection and thanks for after the Communion and I decided I would try to read it myself. Joe Dunne, Davoren's godfather, stood beside me as I read. I quote just a few extracts:

> Thanks to you, Davoren, for giving us so much to celebrate in your short life. You took in the breath of life in powerful gulps often with a great struggle — and gave it back to us in great scoopfuls of love.

> You formed circles of solidarity, of sane and sometimes zany affection, and of warmth and nourishing challenge.

> Thanks to you, Davoren, for your powerful electric presence when Brighid was with us. I will never experience anything in the world as powerful as you in the full ecstasy of communication.

Thank you, Davoren, for your words and poems, sometimes mischievous, often searing and always celebrating the heights and the depths.

Thank you for the brave cheerful years after Brighid was taken from us. You gave us heart when ours, mine and the siblings' and friends', were flagging.

Thank you for continuing to inspire such magic rings of hope and solidarity. You made our house a happy home, witty and irreverent, yet somehow a peaceful haven too.

Thanks and solidarity to all Davoren's fellow-warriors, charioteers and pioneers in disability.

Thanks to you, Davoren, for your puckish spirit. As you lay with us in the house this last day, your cheeky smile still provoked us.

Forgive us, Davoren, for any hardness of heart we may have shown to you.

Thanks to you all — my large and chaotic family — who have loved Davoren and me so joyfully. There was no place for solemn faces in your house, Davoren. Perhaps that is one of your lasting legacies: that there is no place for solemn faces in God's house either.

I want to personally dedicate Davoren's life to the cause of peace in our land. Please God grant us an end to killing and maiming.

Epilogue: Poised for Flight

At the graveside, Paul Coffey played the flute and we all sang 'Kumbaya', which I used to sing beside his bed so often for consolation. "Someone's crying, kumbaya. Someone's laughing, kumbaya. Someone's praying, kumbaya," were some of the refrains I used. We finished with a decade of the Rosary in Irish, led by the parish priest, Fr Earl O'Connor.

As I sit in this room where Davoren slept, where I spent so many hours with him at night, I am still haunted by that phrase, 'poised for flight'. I have listened very carefully to all the different consoling images and formulations that people offered me and respected them all as long as they didn't try to impose them on me. I found very little relief in the idea of Davoren joining his mother, for it offended me to think of happiness for a young man being thought of as linking up with his mother.

Concerning the after-life, I'm an agnostic Christian. I follow the way of negative theology. I have no positive pictures or images. I take very seriously what I learnt as a child: "Eye hath not seen, nor ear heard, what things God hath prepared for those who love him."

I think the mystery of human personality or spirit (call it what you will) shining through our myriad interactions is very deep. Despite Davoren's strictures against me, I would never be a card-carrying member of what he called the "logical negativists". As even Karl Marx observed, taking consolation in a phrase his wife uttered a few days before her death, "We are no such external people." Our stories are part of a larger story. "Earth to earth and dust to dust," we say, but in between, such soaring, such flights, such sorrows, such heart-bonding, such words of nurture and celebration, such song.

Dance on, Davoren.

IV:

Selected Poems

of Davoren Hanna

Contents

Poems in the body of the memoir include: 'Cantata (for Mama)' p. 51, 'Paltry Victory' p. 62, 'Half Loaves' p. 66, 'Utter Tranquility' p. 74, 'Fireworks Whizzardry' p. 80, 'Sacred Spirit' p. 99, 'Two Foxy Scribes' p. 117, and 'Riding Rader Rascally Donkeys' p. 122.

BRIAN

Real comradeship shows in your eyes
as you shake my clenched hand.
Yours are silver-fingered.
They send shivers up the spine
of your clarinet.
The music hungers for hearing.
I will measure out a tune
for you with my folded fists.

GEOGRAPHIC LANDMARKS

The best of all subjects is geography!
Fearsome distances disappear into coloured
shapes like felt-animal jigsaws.
Rivers wriggle like inky worms
across the sellotaped pages of my atlas.
Lakes and mountains nudge each other
sideways as they fight for space
upon my topsy-turvy sandwiched map.
Would Gulliver step on little towns
if the world was as small as this?
Quiet spaces surround me as I ponder,
wide prairies await me when I wander.

FREEWHEELING CHAMP

I listened to the roar
of victory in my ears.
Inch by painful inch
I rode with him —
plummeting downhill,
swerving, gliding,
rising with his wry
Dublin humour
rolling in my spokes.
Satin ribbon roads
slipped under my wheels,
but undaunted came I
to vanquish all doubt
riding in triumph
onto the Champs Elysées.

FUNDERLAND WONDERLAND

Looping the loop was never like this.
Twirling around in space,
watching faces pirouetting
as I list precariously,
my fantastic ship explodes
in a shimmering star-lit memory.

SEAS DAMNED SHALL TAKE THE ARID EARTH BY STORM

in memory of Christy Brown

Feet were made for walking
But not yours — the hell they weren't!
Sun poured through your kinked toes
Whenever the hungry paint licked your soul.
Down all the dancing days of your life,
When incoherence fought with grey uncertainty,
You longed for calloused-handed truth.
Living vibrantly in song and tales of youth,
The dammed up seas of resonance
Shall take the arid earth by storm.

TRAWLER

to my friend Paul, on his thirteenth birthday

Lost in thought,
the little round-eyed cabin boy
gazed into seascapes of dappled grey.
Light trawled the salt-troubled sea
in search of pain-free answers.
When he heard his captain call,
he donned his woolly hat and stood at the helm.
Waves sang a mournful song in his attentive ear.
As tortured sailors loudly cursed their lot,
watch was declared. Hour by white hour went by.
From the depths of barnacled fears
he tugged at manhood's line.
Stout was his fisted tug.

KERRY BOATRIDE

Tenderly my shivering body
was cloaked in sensual warmth
as great frowning mountains
scowled at our night-time frolics.

Shoreline suddenly darkened
as light sneaked slyly away.
Through drizzling tears
I felt the wind's inhospitable enmity.

Reaching a gale-whipped inlet,
our boat huddled in wait.
Lowering a freezing hand
into the choppy waters,

Our boatmen cringed
and muttered an oath.
Cold sank its sharp teeth
into our frail flesh.

Tiny carp floundered in our wake
as churning foam overwhelmed them.
Turning its bows towards land again,
the boat regained its composure.

Three swans sailed by
with stealthy beauty,
ribboning the dark water
with white aplomb.

Twisting my frozen cheek
in their direction,
I saw light breaking
through their ruffled wings.

TOM SAWYER, EAT YOUR HEART OUT!

I grimaced in pain.
Freed from my bonds
of muscle-tightening mother stricture,
I worshipped at the shrine of boyhood.
The light was Burmese-brown
on the brackish river.
The frail craft bobbed wildly
on the swirling water.
It made torrential queasy womenfolk
faint with fear at our intrepidity.
Each rapid overcome,
we plunged over the precipice
of questioning adolescence,
leaving Huckleberry Finn
to row back to the shore.

SATURDAY BLUES

Sallying forth we braved the biting wind
brashly hawking its winter wares.
Chill were asperity's long fingers
touching my tender cheeks.

Grey my thoughts and grey my heart
as we roved in search of solace:
"Come home and sit beside my soul,
my friend, and let me hear you sing."

Alas, friend, my tongue is bound
with the Fates' infernal string.
Should you care to hold a strand
we can loosen its lethal grip.

And should you find slight tension
as the knots untangle, friend,
wrap your strong arms round me
till we reach the ravelled end.

BIRTH HIDDEN FROM AN UNCARING WORLD

He came forth
breech-birthed.

Stars wept
when they heard
the Virgin scream
and blood filled the sky.

Safe delivery hurried,
Joseph cut the grief-cord.
He lies severed now
from her frail flesh.

Child reddened
by history's blood sacrifice,
do you ever ask yourself
why me?

MY LIFE, MY VOICE, MY STORY

The moon blackened at my birth
and long night's cry began.
Pain became my bed-fellow
and despair my song.
God disappeared behind the clouds;
I lost my star-signpost to hope.

Light found a chink to peep through
when poems were read to my starved soul.
Loneliness brought moments of repose;
lines poured through my veins
and love glimmered on my tongue.
Little birds became my inspiration.

Left with my own silent melody,
I painted notes of long-forgotten tunes
trembling in my trapped heart.
Light burst through my dark mouth
and myriad songs flew heavenwards.
I was poised for flight . . .

GETHSEMANE

Sentenced, punished, parodied —
we live in a grey habitat
as light denies us hope.
The great garden blooms anew
but no purpose have we here
fixed like stakes to the budding rose
nay, riveted to Christ's calvary-tree.

FIREBIRDS
to Cian

We are insurrection survivors.
Rising when the ashes have cooled,
we spread our tremulous wings.
Reeling from the acrid smoke of burnt dreams,
we soar — none the worse for having scattered
great illusory schemes into fragments
which float mirthlessly in the glowing sky.
Going lustily into battle we had little to lose,
now we have myriad flight-paths to travel
    together.

SCALLYWAG MOGGY HAIKU

Whiskers askew,
she ascends the tree
bent on bird-scaring.
Awful cat!

THE FRIENDSHIP TREE

There springs water, sweet water,
in my parched little plot;
greenly my soul shoots
till it brushes heaven's underbelly.

ANNETTE

Tiny grains of fine sand
trouble the oyster in his shell,
yet look what rich harvest comes forth.
Touched by your gentle beauty,
my solitary seed grows luminous
and bursts its constraining bonds.

NATIVITY

to my friend Brendan

As you knelt at my feet
I saw tears in your heart.
At my birth no comets lit the cold sky;
loss shall be my gold, frankincense and myrrh.
Letting tears fall on the thin straw
at the sight of manhood blighted,
like Veronica, you looked into my eyes
and whispered "Why?"

CIRCLINGS

to Máire

Flying higher than the peregrine
on his silver wing,
your voice skims the contours
of the universe.

It hums over hilly heather clusters,
gently caressing their eager
purple lips stained with the
full-bodied bouquet of your notes.

Nestling in the crevasses
of my silent flesh,
your song nuzzles my spirit
and I dance.

BRENDAN

Pleasure knew no bounds when we met —
that grey-faced afternoon on the cobbles
of majestic learning's playground;
poetic language cannot describe
my fellow-feeling flight towards Danaë
as I savoured your sensitive being.

LIFT THE EDGES
for Barry

Licked by salt-silvered streams of unshed tears,
my cheeks crave grief-channels where agony can lie.
Selfish sorrows need not linger long
since they nick but few notches in my sapling bark.
Grief bites into my bole and lodges in knots
of silent gall, dulling my raging soul.
Green furrows, lift your edges and valley my tears.

LILIES AND DAFFODILS

in memory of Jenny, died
February 1989, aged four

Bone-white —
she left prints
of her pale feet
upon their wasted land.
Breathless she lay
at dove-dawn.

Why ruby the clouds
with your grief?
Look instead upon
her sunkissed daffodil
flaunting its yellow
death-defying head.

GREEN SECRETS

for Mary Condren on her father's death

Fresh daisies evoke your spirit —
green fragile stalk, heavy head,
grief-golden heart, listless leaves;
dancing fronds on the underside
of your festive nature drooping,
because fine fathering has ended.
Heart, rinse your girlish centre —
weep, raindrops, weep.

FAMINE

Woven banks of weeds
pay their last respects
to rank potato stalks —
now razed and ravaged
by hungry folk.
Lamentation purples
the tepid wind,
tingeing it with dolour.
Tormented corpses fill
the maw of the famine crucible.
A small boy stands still —
astounded to be there.

ETHIOPIAN DANCE

Young wasted faces ask,
"Who has let this happen?
Who has willed to apathetic posterity
this legacy of mordant hunger
and anguished moans?"
Quiescent, weak and bereft of dignity,
they turn in hope to others,
while the silent *pas de deux* with death
continues for countless more.

HOLOCAUST

Only hell can have been more horrific
as lines of skeletal angels fell
from the grace of one called Hitler.
Grimly gesturing towards the steady throng,
the sentinel of death allocated chambers.
Sepia ran the earth with the blood
of the sons and daughters of Zion.
Weep, O weep, all you who love humanity.

LAMENT FOR SHOSTAKOVICH

for Philip Breen

O taste his blood . . .
His sojourned soul
was doubly clubbed
by ruthless regimes.
Wrath-handed notes fought
with his melodic spirit.
Aloe-black tears rivulate down
stark landscapes of iron.
They wash mountainous indifference away.

CELAN EVENING

Free-wheeling stars spin red ecstasy
into my parched well.
Wise man, you weighed down words
in your pocket of droughted dreams
as you sang your sad death-song.

THE APPRENTICE BARD

for Seamus Heaney

He digs also 'man'
or perhaps 'woman'.
Since he cannot even hold a pen —
never mind a workman's spade —
what trove can he unearth
this side of infinity?

'Poète célèbre' that you are,
would that I too could sing
like songbirds of your ilk.

Yevtushenko and I have met once before
in the scrawny days of our apprenticeship.
When the gods of art
bestowed their praise on me,
like Yevgeni I ran shouting in the streets.

HOW THE EARTH WAS FORMED QUIZ

What does a volcano do?
It sends Pliny the Roman naturalist
rushing to Vesuvius's gaping jaw
in search of its scarlet secret.
And how was the earth's crust formed?
Heaven's master-baker,
Lord of holocausts and light,
touched his dough with fingers of fire
and then sighed upon it.
And do lines of latitude run north to south?
Why, a swallow's heart-quickening
will tell the way home to his haven
whatever way the lines are drawn.

I ASK BUT FOR THE DIVINER'S WAND

Pleats, stumps, loam —
words like these are clay-bound.
When I search for glimmering sounds
I scan the skies hoping
to harvest love-knots.
Ploughing the depths,
I turn up the bedrock clay.
I home into water
but waste such precious hours
treasure-hunting the juicy soil.
A sally rod twitches —
water stirs in the gathered
folds of the earth's petticoat —
would that I too had the diviner's wand.

DEATH OF A SPACE SHUTTLE

The pinnacle of fame, lightning-struck.
Perhaps round-shouldered Atlas grew weary
and dropped his orb upon their frail craft.
Salvage, O salvage their dreams, Lord,
as you enfold them in your vast canopy.

They did not leave deep treatises
on the meaning of the universe.
No, theirs was a greater legacy —
a waltz among the stars with death's armament
freely spinning in a sunless shrieking sky.

THE DANCING BEAR

November 1989

Festivities will never stop at Berlin's wall.
Streets that were once lugubrious grey
now entangle as lovers do through
the long-limbed summer nights.
Seeking admission to the nuptial feast,
flesh once striped by searchlight-beams
now dances arm in arm with comrades
on the other side of freedom's wall.
Slow caravans of eager immigrants
bring knapsacked hopes in their hearts.
Light kindles the naked callous stones
and luminous dreams mutate the skies.

THE SUMMER THE CAMERA CREW CAME TO THE
ISLAND OF LEROS

PLOT: grovelling committee members
of the bin marked 'human garbage'
send overdue cries for help
from medieval squalor
to the heights of Mount Media.

CHARACTERS: nameless nobodies
with no sign of hope
in their blank staring eyes.

LOCATION: Leros asylum interior —
no furniture, no costumes, no action,
lighting murky, dialogue none.

COMMENTARY: no need to understand Greek,
official translation given
(text mislaid) —
all rights of man violated —
no copyright.

SACERDOTAL SPRING

It is fragility that intrigues me —
the limp hand that shakes mine,
the great hollow-eyed head
of the newborn foal
who staggers unsteadily
on spindly legs.
I have touched the feeble stamens
of a wilting crocus
and trembled in deference
to such decaying beauty.
The fragility of God's hold
on our cavernous hearts
threatens to shake the blossom of our faith.
But listen! the Priest of Love
still sings in purple ecstasy.

SAPLING BENT BY A CRUEL WIND

Awful asymmetry;
wheeled and twisted children—
love's foolhardy moment
soldered into frail flesh—
tacitly I watch them
slide into oblivion
as their dreams freeze
in the bitter barren air.
Who has ordained it so?
By what legerdemain
did such lamentation
befall the innocent?
When almost all creatures
beget their kind,
whither our benighted tribe?

ODE TO MAMA

I was fortunate to have
travelled all over
the wide world arena
with you as my serial music teacher;
sweet-sounding sempiternal
melodies peal in my ears
whenever you tell me
a tale of Pericles or Beowulf.

SALLY FORTH

Go, father, out to dig
the embittered earth.
Take the unwilling season
in your grasp and blow
upon its frozen finger.
Pluck the dead twigs
from winter's tired embrace
and see how nature
girds her girlish loins
ready and excitedly
in wait for you.

PRAYER FOR MY PARENTS

Lord, life is like a segment of an orange.
The piece I got is dry and full of pips.
Biting it, the bitter fruit sears my tongue
and no sounds issue from my wounded lips.
When I received my portion, my gift I spat
in your holy face, so woeful was my lot.
Then liquid love enfolded me as parents
beheld my disappointment and my grief.
Their lot indeed was hard for them to bear,
no half-measures did they give me either
but filled my bone-dry soul to overflowing
from the bountiful juice of their care.
Lord, no greater parents could a child have,
such love is denied many and is rare.

FALCON

Plummeting into grey,
the falcon swerved
to touch the water
as time took a breath.
I heard his cry
and saw the glint of hope
in his grieving feathers.
Father, you grow wise
in your search for truth.
But real truth remains
hidden behind the grin
you wear in childhood photographs
still fixed limply
to dry reason's wall.
Soar, father, soar.

LINES IN TIME OF GREAT HAPPINESS

Ploughman, you can never know
the pleasure of seafaring
straddled as you are
across the earth's brown back.
Were I to sail upon the crest
of happiness surging in my heart
clay thoughts would crumble
and my harrowed tongue be freed.